Endorsements

"The Mestas family by faith stepped into the Miracle of Adoption, and with their story of hope, this story will encourage and challenge many on the same journey."
—**Mary Beth Chapman, President of Show Hope**

"Eileen and Jerry Mestas have drunk deeply of both the joy and the pain that so often come intertwined as we embrace the distress of the orphan. In *More Than "I" Can Handle*, the rest of us get a small taste of that joy and pain also in the tumultuous experiences, surprising delights and deep insights of their story. Perhaps few adoptive families will have a journey as unconventional as the Mestases, but all stand to learn much from them. And while not everyone may hold the same opinions as the Mestases on every issue, none can deny the compelling beauty of the family that has sprung up from their self-giving love."
—**Jedd Medefind, President, Christian Alliance for Orphans**

"*More Than "I" Can Handle* is not just an inspiring story about adoption, it is the story of a family transformed by obedience to God's promises. Don't just be inspired. Be challenged to answer the question, 'How can God's promises to orphans be fulfilled through my family?' Eileen is proof that He can do more than you could possibly imagine."
—**Tom Davis, CEO, Children's HopeChest**

"*More Than "I" Can Handle* is an accurate depiction of the tangibility of GOD in adoption. This 'REAL' experience, as told the way only Eileen could tell it, provokes laughter and tears, victory and pain, joy and sadness. Honesty reigns and JESUS prevails in this story, and the reality that if we choose to listen … we WILL hear Him."
—**Carolyn Twietmeyer, Founder/Executive Director,**
  Project HOPEFUL, nfp

D1496102

Endorsements

"WOW! ... is what I found myself saying as I turned each page. You will see great faith of this family, in an even more faithful God! Crazy? Yes. Real? Yes. Miracles? Yes!"
—Andy Lehman, Vice President, Lifesong for Orphans
   Board Member, Christian Alliance for Orphans

"I could not put this book down! I was enthralled by the amount of faith that the Mestas family has in the Lord. They do not allow anyone or anything to stand in their way when He calls them to do something! As I turned each page, I found myself in awe of just how mighty our God is. Their story has inspired me to risk more for Christ, because He is faithful to guide us through the risk. If you have a heart for reaching the fatherless, this book is a must-read!"
—Hayley Catt, Photographer and
   Web-Coordinator for the films *Fireproof* and *Courageous*

"Never have I been so challenged and encouraged to walk by faith. The Mestas family has learned the value of obedience when the odds were stacked against them, and they have watched the Lord fulfill His promises over and over again in their lives. Your heart will be riveted as you follow their journey to embrace the orphans of the world as the Father does. Eileen's book is an honest, compelling story with a miracle on every page."
—Meredith Andrews, Dove Award-Winning
   Contemporary Music Artist

"Eileen Mestas is a fiery fiesta of faith. What separates her from other believers is that she not only hears but acts! Her obedience to the sweet whisper of the Holy Spirit is the tool God has used to write this amazing story. Read on and your faith will be inspired, fed and rewarded."
—Jodi Jackson Tucker, International Director, Orphan Sunday

Endorsements

"AMAZING is the word to describe the story of how an amazing God has worked in the hearts and lives of a pair of very ordinary people, Jerry and Eileen Mestas. Eileen shares their story with such concise accuracy and refreshing honesty that you won't want to put this testimony down. Reader, beware—you may laugh and you may weep, but you surely will be inspired and challenged by the God Who is a father to the fatherless."
—Fran Idziak, Bible Study Instructor with
Precept Ministries International

"The Mestas family story is truly amazing and inspiring! Their story reminds us of a tremendous need in the world, but also of a God whose provision is sufficient when we trust and obey. Too often, believers see a need and assume that nothing can be done. But God has provoked the Mestases to take action, and shown His grace to them as they pour out their lives for His children. I'm hopeful that believers will listen to this story and begin thinking about how God might use them to bless those who have no hope."
—James K. Dew, Jr., PhD, Dean of the College,
Southeastern Baptist Theological Seminary, Wake Forest, NC

I pray this
story will encourage
you in faith to trust and
obey the Lord Jesus Christ on
the journey He has for you and your
family. I pray His richest blessings
upon you! Jeremiah 29:11-13
In His Timing + Care,
Eileen Mestas
Jerry Mestas
James 1:27

Jeremiah :)

James :)

Josiah
Keziah
Keren

MORE THAN "I" CAN HANDLE

one family's story of trusting God
through the impossible

Eileen Mestas

WINTERS PUBLISHING

P.O. Box 501
Greensburg, IN 47240
812-663-4948
www.WintersPublishing.com

Table of Contents

Introduction

Now to him who is able to do immeasurably more than all we ask or imagine, according to his power that is at work within us, to him be glory in the church and in Christ Jesus throughout all generations, for ever and ever! Amen (Ephesians 3:20-21).

I am just an ordinary, middle-aged woman who loves the Lord Jesus Christ and is striving to live my life for His purpose and His glory. One day I realized how perfectly my name fits me—Eileen "I lean" on the Lord 'cuz I'm a "messed up" Mestas! I am Jerry's wife, and Mama to eight beautiful and amazing children—Melissa, Jonathan, Ellie, James, Jeremiah, Josiah, Keren, and Keziah. I am also Grandma to Vaden, Cana, and Callum, and mother-in-law to Randy. I am a sister, daughter, and friend. But most importantly, I am a sinner who has committed every sin imaginable and realized I needed a Savior, the Lord Jesus Christ, the only One who could save me from the path to hell. By His grace I am a forgiven child of God and daughter of the King. I am a work in progress, and trust in the power of the Holy Spirit to complete the work He has begun in me to accomplish all He has planned for my life.

I was born and raised in New York, in a blue-collar, middle-class family. My parents were very loving and dedicated to raising happy and responsible children. We were Catholic, but were not a churchgoing family. All of my life, I have had a hunger for God and a desire to know Him. So I spent most of my childhood going to church alone, seeking to spend time with Him, but never being intentionally taught the Word of God. Mom stayed home, raising us four kids until we got older, when she gradually went from part-time to full-time employment in a variety of jobs. While they had many struggles over the years, my parents were committed to family and each other, celebrating fifty-four years of marriage, when my father died in 2009. I always loved school; I was an honor student and have always been a social butterfly. While in high school, I attended BOCES trade school and graduated in 1977, with my first career planned as a certified Dental Assistant. I have had several career changes since then, with my favorite being a wife and full-time stay at home mom.

When I was sixteen, I fell in love with my high school sweetheart and planned to live happily ever after as husband and wife. But, like most relationships that begin when we are young, naive, and immature, it broke my heart and turned into a disaster. I was so in love with him that I gave myself wholeheartedly, including my virginity. We were together for two years and I thought he was just as committed and in love as I was. But it turned out he was seeing other girls behind my back, and was making other plans. When I found out I was pregnant, I was plagued with fear and lies. When I told him, he was adamant that we should have an abortion. After all, it was just a blob of tissue and no one would be hurt. This was the common belief back then. Because of my ignorance of the Word of God, and what I was taught by my parents' worldview, my health classes in school and the culture of my day, I believed this was merely an inconvenience and that abortion was not only acceptable, but the "right choice," considering the circumstances. While deep in my heart I felt this was wrong; I succumbed to the peer pressure and lies, thinking I had no other choice, and I had an abortion. Soon after, my boyfriend ended our relationship and joined the military.

I was devastated and kept telling myself I had done the right thing. I wanted to live in denial of the sin I had committed, but I had a deep pain in my heart. I began to cry out to God to take control of my life, because I knew I was not making wise choices, and I did not want to continue on that path. Because of my selfishness and distorted worldview, I committed the sin of murder. This is something I live with and grieve over every day, and wish I could go back for a "do over." It took many years, but I eventually realized and admitted that the child that was inside of me was not a blob of tissue; it was a real person, created in the image of God.

With the popularity and practice of using ultrasound machines, it has been proven that life begins at conception, and it is a real baby! It became especially clear to me when I became a mother in 1983. At eighteen weeks' gestation, I had an ultrasound, and saw my baby sucking her thumb and very clearly looking like a real baby.

As I began to study God's Word, I learned *For you created my inmost being; you knit me together in my mother's womb. I praise you because I am fearfully and wonderfully made; your works are wonderful, I know that full well (Psalm 139:13-14).*

It is only because of the revelation of my guilt and sin, and true repentance, that I have received forgiveness from the Lord Jesus. I share this testimony with hope that it may save someone else from making the same mistake, or from living with the guilt and pain of regret. The Lord is in the business of restoring the years the locusts have eaten, and He is a God of second chances. It is because of my sin that I can't handle this life without the Savior to rescue me from the pit of hell. He has restored my soul and given me the hope that, in spite of who I am, He still has plans for my life, with a hope and future to do good. God gave me the love of my life, and Jerry and I just celebrated the miracle of thirty-three years of marriage. It has been one wild ride! We were married on August 11, 1979, with great hopes, dreams and aspirations that our lives would be full of love, laughter, family, and lots of happy memories. I was nineteen years old and he was twenty-seven, with a well-established career as a police officer with the Los Angeles Police Department.

On May 3, 1979, Jerry and I met at a motel in Phoenix, Arizona, while I was sitting at the pool reading my Bible. I was traveling with my sister and her husband, who were moving there, and I was going to travel on for another two weeks to visit a girlfriend who was attending college in California. He was there on his first day of a month-long vacation, to attend the "Pig Bowl," which was a football game between the LAPD and the Arizona State Police. We all spent several hours talking at the pool, and then he invited me to go with him to the game the following day. We spent the entire weekend talking and having meals together. My plan was to take a bus to California that Sunday morning, and he was planning to drive back to California, then leave with a friend for a two-week vacation in Mexico.

As Providence would have it, he offered to take me to my girlfriend's house, since it was on his way home. When we got there, I was shocked to find that she had changed, and was not the same girl she was back home. She greeted us in the parking lot, looking very strange. When I asked her if she was all right, she told me she had just taken some drugs to get high, and that she was having a party to celebrate my arrival. She had no idea I was sitting in the car with two LAPD officers who were on vacation! Jerry helped take my luggage to her apartment, and there were several people there, drinking and obviously high. I immediately asked him to turn around and take me to the airport. This was not the girl I knew, and I was not going to stay there for two weeks. We went outside to talk, and Jerry said he did not want me to leave before getting the chance to see California. He suggested I go stay at his parents' house. His younger sister was my age and she had an empty bed in her room. My response was, "I don't even know you; I can't go stay with your family!" As it turned out, I told my friend to send everyone home so we could talk, and that I was leaving in the morning. I was a real party crasher! We talked for a long time and I begged her to change her lifestyle before it was too late. Jerry promised to pick me up in the morning and take me to the airport. Later that evening, he called me and we talked on the phone until the sun came up. He was concerned about leaving me there and wanted to be sure I was safe.

A few hours later, Jerry picked me up and we went to breakfast. He told me he had cancelled his vacation to Mexico and did not want me to leave. He asked me to stay for the two weeks and he would take me sightseeing all over California. After prayer and consulting my family, I decided to stay. The first day, he took me to his parents' house to meet all of his family, who were very welcoming. He is one of thirteen children and the house was full of love and laughter. They knew he had cancelled his trip because of me and figured there must be something very special going on. He took me to Disneyland, Universal Studios, and all the famous sights in the Los Angeles area. He even took me to visit his family in Fresno and to see the sights of San Francisco. After two weeks of spending every waking moment together and talking about everything under the sun, it was time for me to go home. That's when he asked if he could go with me. He still had two more weeks of vacation and had always wanted to visit New York. We had been communicating with my family, and they were excited for him to come home with me so they could meet him. We had another two weeks of spending every waking hour together, seeing all the sights of NYC, and my family really liked him too.

A few days before he was to leave, he went to my father and asked for my hand in marriage. I was shocked when my father called me into a meeting to ask if I was interested in accepting his proposal. I will never forget his words, "I know you don't know each other for a long time; but we really like him, he has a good career, and when he looks at you there is love in his eyes. I think you should accept." I too had fallen in love with him, and felt peace that this was the man I was to marry. He came from a good family, he had a good job, we were both raised Catholic, and had the same foundational beliefs. Needless to say, we had a whirlwind of a romance and we were married two months later.

I left my family and my "country," and moved to California to begin my life as a new bride. I felt like I was going to a foreign land where I had no roots or family of my own. They even speak a different language. His family was very loving toward me and I felt like I was adopted into the family. I was very happy and thought our life together was going to be perfect.

While we were trying to live a righteous life, both of us were ignorant of God's Word, and began navigating our lives based on worldly wisdom, and selfish, sinful desires. Scattered among seasons of incredible blessings have been extremely difficult times, including struggles with alcohol abuse, infidelity, financial crisis, infertility, anger, resentment, and unforgiveness.

After eleven years together, we were separated and headed for divorce. I had given up all hope and truly believed our marriage was over. We had become two separate people, living separate lives under one roof, and I was bitter and angry. This was not what I had signed up for, not what I had hoped, dreamed and worked so hard for. I was trying to do everything I could think of to make a happy home, and it seemed like the more I tried, the worse it got. I finally gave up all hope and wanted a divorce. It even got to the point that a divorce was not good enough. I still had to deal with him and the other women that would be in his life, because we had a child together. In my sinful and selfish mind, the best solution was if he would get killed on the job. I am not proud of where I was emotionally; I am just being real and honest, because God knew my heart and thoughts at all times.

On Christmas Day in 1988, Jerry asked if he could come

to church with me and Melissa. We had started going to a non-denominational Christian church after Melissa started attending an AWANA program there. He attended several times and decided he liked it. For the first time, he understood that he was a sinner and needed Jesus as his Savior. He dedicated his life to Jesus Christ, becoming a born-again believer. He repented and asked me for forgiveness for all he had done to hurt me and destroy our marriage. But I went to my pastor and told him that I wanted a divorce because I had legal grounds according to the Scriptures, and I had no feelings for Jerry anymore. I thought it was too late to reconcile, and that Jerry was just going through the motions of trying to get us back, but was not sincere. My pastor said if Jerry really was born again, his life would change and he would become the man/husband that I had always wanted. If I did not stay with him, someone else would reap the benefits of all my hard work and suffering through this difficult marriage. Then came the kick in the gut, as he read this Scripture, *"For if you forgive men when they sin against you, your heavenly Father will also forgive you. But if you do not forgive men their sins, your Father will not forgive your sins: (Matthew 6:14)*. He said Jerry had repented and asked for my forgiveness, and I had to give him another chance. It took awhile, but I was convicted, and realized that I too had responsibility in our marriage failing. I realized I could not really know Jerry's heart and intentions, but I did know I could trust God. I had to obey the Lord and put all my trust and faith in Him alone. Only He had the power to really change both of us to do the work necessary to restore our relationship. My other motivation was my baby girl, Melissa, who adored her papa. She was going through agony, because she loved us both and was being emotionally abused by the whole ugly situation. I was heartbroken for her and wanted to do everything I could to make her happy. I honestly believed that this was my cross to bear, and that I had to go back to my marriage out of obedience to God, but not because "I wanted to."

I decided to take a leap of faith as I heard the Lord whispering, *"Trust Me!"* It was time to trust Him with my life and my marriage. I pictured it like jumping out of a plane with a parachute on my back for the first time, strapped to the expert skydiver (Jesus Christ), hoping and trusting He would get me safely to the ground.

I was and still am a faithful listener of *Focus on the Family* radio broadcast, and for the first time in my life I heard testimonies of people who had gone through these same trials and were successfully reconciled, because they gave total control of their lives to God. Dr. Dobson's book *Love Must Be Tough* and his radio programs also gave me hope and practical tools to walk through this journey to healing and restoration.

Thus began the miraculous reconciliation of our marriage, and our lives have been an exciting and amazing testimony of faith and trustworthiness to the Lord's grace, mercy, and forgiveness ever since. Praise God that He broke us and showed us how to surrender all to Him. Jerry finally realized he had really lost his family; he wanted it back. He made intentional choices to change his behavior and rebuild trust in our marriage. I too had to make major changes in my behavior and expectations. While we are still a work in progress, we are not the same people, and God has proven faithful to do more than we could have ever imagined or hoped for. We learned that "love is a choice," and God is the healer and restorer of relationships. Jerry and I are more in love today than we have ever been. There is not a day that goes by that we look at all God has done in our lives, and we are grateful that we were obedient to work through our difficulties. We couldn't imagine missing out on the wonderful life we have today.

After dedicating our lives and renewing our marriage commitment to Jesus Christ and one another, Melissa was also saved, and we were baptized as a family. We fell in love with the church, the Word of God, and our journey to a new life as born-again believers. We were blessed with two more children, Jonathan and Ellie, and were living a happy, comfortable life in Southern California.

In 1994, Jerry retired from the Los Angeles Police Department after twenty years of service, and we felt led by the Lord to make a fresh start and move our family to North Carolina. Jerry took a job as an insurance investigator and we settled down to the business of raising children, serving in the church, and enjoying the laid-back charm of small-town Southern living. Life was good! Little did we know that the Lord was about to turn our lives upside down and inside out! First, in 1995, He called us to homeschool our children. I hadn't planned on this. Me? Homeschool? What about socialization?

How will they get into college? I had all the typical worries and concerns about my qualifications for this new venture, but the Lord was whispering, *"Trust Me."*

Then, in 2003, God convicted us that we were to trust Him for the size of our family and begin a journey to adoption. Again, doubts filled my mind. Could I really love an adopted child as much as I loved my three biological children? Could we provide financially for a bigger family the way that we wanted? The Lord spoke a little louder, *"Trust Me."* In 2004, we suddenly found ourselves unemployed. Jerry found temporary employment here and there, but he ended up working only three of the next six years. We had added two new babies to the family and my aging parents had recently moved into our home as well. Our savings account was quickly wiped out and I found myself lying wide awake in bed at night, arguing with God. "Where are You? Why would You do this to us? What if we lose our house?" Over and over again, I felt the Lord's presence and heard His reassuring voice saying, *"Trust Me."* Unbelievably, in the midst of this time, the Lord seemed to be calling us to grow our family AGAIN, this time through international adoption. Now, this didn't make any sense at all! I was forty-nine years old and Jerry was pushing fifty-five! We were too old! Besides, international adoption is very expensive, and we had NO MONEY! We already had five children, Jerry had only just recently started a new job, and we had no savings! What in the world? Were we insane? I'm sure some people thought so (and probably still do)! But once again, the Lord spoke to our hearts with these words, *"Trust Me."*

There is a saying that God doesn't give us more than we can handle. Well, I know that isn't true! God says He will not let us be tempted more than we can bear (1 Corinthians 10:13), but it does not say we will be able to handle everything that happens in life on our own. The Lord has definitely given me way more than "I" can handle—on my own. The truth is that I would be a basket case were it not for the One who strengthens me (Philippians 4:13). It is the power of the Holy Spirit and His Word that gives me the ability to handle everything in my life. My loving heavenly Father arms me with strength (2 Samuel 22:33) to accomplish His will on a minute by minute basis. His grace is sufficient for me, for His power is made perfect in my weakness. *Therefore, I will boast all the more gladly about my weaknesses, so that Christ's power may rest on me (2 Corinthians 12:9).*

The Bible is full of stories about people who were called to do things they couldn't handle. Moses was called to ask mighty Pharaoh to grant freedom to all the Israelite slaves, but he begged God to find someone else, because he didn't feel equal to the task. Joshua was called to defeat the great walled city of Jericho by marching his army in circles around it, and the people standing on the walls laughed. Gideon was called to lead the Israelites against the much bigger and stronger Midianite army, and he threw out a fleece, not once, but twice, to be sure that he was hearing God correctly. Jesus' disciples were instructed to feed a hungry crowd of 5,000 people with a measly two loaves of bread and seven fish, and they tried to convince Him to send the people elsewhere. But in each case, God's plan was greater than what man could see from his limited perspective. It is when God calls us to do things that we know we cannot handle that He has the opportunity to show us His incredible love, mercy, grace, and mighty power. And in those times, we have the opportunity to grow in faith and we fall even deeper in love with Him. *For we are God's workmanship, created in Christ Jesus to do good works, which God prepared in advance for us to do (Ephesians 2:10).*

The Lord has given me a story to tell about the miraculous signs, wonders, and provision our family experienced when we began to listen, trust, and obey His voice, even when it didn't make sense. I am blessed with more than I deserve; more children, more joy, more love, more happiness, and more faith. I pray that tHIS story will encourage you to be faithful to listen, trust, and obey whatever God is calling you to do in your life. There is another saying—God doesn't call the equipped, but He equips those He calls—and I do believe that! It is only by His will that I write this book of testimony for His purpose and His glory. I have come to understand that my life is not my own. It is not about me! It is truly more than "I" can handle, which is why I have bowed my knee and surrendered my life to the Almighty God who never gives me more than HE can handle!

1 From Fear to Trust

Sons are a heritage from the LORD, children a reward from him. Like arrows in the hands of a warrior are sons born in one's youth. Blessed is the man whose quiver is full of them ... (Psalm 127:3-5).

When we were dating, Jerry and I discussed the idea of having three or four children and then adopting one or two after that. He is one of thirteen children, I am one of four, and we both love big families! After we got married, we decided not to use birth control and it was three years before our first born, Melissa, came into the world. We were ecstatic! This baby girl brought tremendous love and joy into our lives, and by the time she was two years old, we were ready to welcome another little bundle of joy. When Melissa was five and we still hadn't gotten pregnant, we realized there must be a problem. At the time, I was working full-time in the corporate world, while juggling the responsibilities of being a wife and mother. I enjoyed my job, but I was conflicted because I also wanted to be home with my baby! We just didn't see how it was financially possible, and as a result, I was stressed to the max.

My obstetrician, who was also an infertility specialist, put us through every possible test. When all the tests came back normal, the next recommendation was artificial insemination. The whole family, including my daughter and my parents, was involved and supportive in our quest for fertility, helping with babysitting, charting temperatures, and moral support. When we still weren't able to produce a pregnancy, the final procedure was to take the prescribed fertility drug, Clomid. After the maximum allotted time and no results, my doctor called us in for a final consultation to say there was nothing more he could do, and I was being released as his patient. He told me that God is in control of making babies, and he only had the ability to fix something that was broken. Since he could find no physical problems and the fertility procedures and medication didn't work, it was now between us and God.

This was also during the season our marriage began to show signs of trouble. Initially, I didn't realize just how bad it was going to get and I had hoped that if we got pregnant, things would get better. As I look back now, and hindsight gives 20/20 vision, I thank the Lord that He knew what was best for us and did not give us a child then. Unbeknownst to us, we had several years of work to do, including salvation, before we were ready to begin growing a healthy family.

Since we found ourselves unable to have more children the conventional way, we decided that maybe God was calling us to grow our family through adoption. This was something that we had discussed back when we were dating. We did not want Melissa to be an only child, so we started working with Bethany Christian Services, and after a few months we were selected by a birth mother, pregnant with twins. We were so excited! A few months later, I got sick with what I thought was the flu, but a visit to the doctor determined that I was, in fact, pregnant! We were absolutely shocked! It had been several years since we had worked with the fertility specialist and I honestly thought I could never get pregnant again. When we told our case worker at Bethany, she said we had to be released from the program because at that time they only worked with infertile couples. We were very disappointed, but looked forward to welcoming the new baby growing in my womb, and trusted that God had everything in control!

I was back as a patient with my OB/fertility doctor. This pregnancy was difficult, and I started going into labor at five months. During this difficult time, God protected Jonathan and he was born healthy, a month early, in June 1990. We didn't know if we'd ever be able to get pregnant again, but rejoiced that God had given us two beautiful children. Then two years later, God gave us an unexpected surprise. I was shocked to discover I was pregnant again without even trying. I decided to break the news to everyone on Christmas

Eve, 1992; I gave Jerry and the kids a special card. They opened it and read, "Congratulations on your new baby!" At first they were confused, thinking I had put the wrong card in the envelope, but then the realization of what they had read dawned on them, and they too were shocked. Everyone jumped up and down with joy as we shared the good news. We were all delighted the Lord had seen fit to bless us with our third child, Ellie, born in August 1993, healthy and beautiful. For years, we had been intentionally praying for the blessing of children, and now we had three!

In 1994, the Lord took us on another new adventure, moving across country from California to North Carolina, and for the first time in our lives we were far from family and friends. I began to fear what would happen if I got pregnant again. All three of my pregnancies had been difficult, and we had depended greatly on our family for support. Who would help with the kids if I got pregnant now? What if I required bed rest again? My mom had always told me that two children, a boy and a girl, made a perfect family. The world tells us that children are very expensive and difficult to raise—just wait until those teenage years! What about college? We were middle-aged now. Convincing ourselves that it made sense to be finished having children, we scheduled a vasectomy, believing that our little family was complete.

As we left the doctor's office following the procedure, both Jerry and I immediately felt ashamed, like Adam and Eve in the Garden, when they realized they were naked. Fear and lies had taken root in our hearts and we strayed from seeking the Lord's will for our family. Everything I read in the Bible about children says they are a blessing, a gift, an inheritance from the Lord. It never calls them too expensive or a burden! We were convicted and pleaded with God to forgive us for not trusting Him. A glimmer of hope came from stories we had heard of unsuccessful vasectomies. Jerry never made the follow-up appointment to verify if the procedure was a success, and we agreed never to tell anyone what we had done. Hoping against hope, we started to pray for more children.

How quickly we fall away from trusting God and believing His Word. The Bible tells about many people who walked with God and then turned away from trusting Him. Abraham. David. Peter. The good news is that God still used these people in spite of their failures. One night, I couldn't sleep. I felt the urge to meet with the Lord, so I got up and went to get my Bible. I began to pray and read through His Word. I felt like God was telling me that He had a plan for me, He knew how many children He would send us, and when and how. *"Trust Me."* I felt impressed in my heart that He was telling me *"I am going to give you a son and you are to name him Jeremiah."* I began to cry and went to my journal, writing down my thoughts because I felt so strongly I was in the presence of the Lord. I called a family meeting that evening and shared what I had heard from God. Melissa, a senior in high school, said, "No, Mama! You are too old. This can't be true!" We talked and talked, and ultimately decided that if God was going to send us a son, it would be a miracle and we would rejoice and be grateful. We weren't sure how it would happen, but we were ready to surrender again and trust God with control of our family.

2 Homeschool— Not Me!

Ever since I started seriously asking God to take control of my life, He has gently been transforming all facets of it. Psalm 111:10 says, *The fear of the LORD is the beginning of wisdom; all who follow his precepts have good understanding.* As I study my Bible, I find understanding about how to handle each new day and each new situation, and the Lord is faithful to answer my prayers and direct us down the path He has chosen specifically for me and for my family.

After God resurrected our marriage, I began to intentionally seek His wisdom on how to be a better wife. After He gave us children, I did the same, seeking wisdom on how to be a better mother. I knew that God's instruction and wisdom are found in His Word, so I dove into Bible study and prayer, both on my own, and in local groups such as community Bible study and Precept Ministries. Matthew 5:6 says, *"Blessed are those who hunger and thirst for righteousness, for they will be filled."* I learned so much, and the more I learned, the more I wanted to know! As I grew in understanding, I also learned to listen for God's voice speaking directly to me—that nudge in my spirit, that burden on my heart that won't go away. And as I learned to hear His voice, I also learned to obey and follow Him. This is something I am still striving to do on a daily and minute by minute basis.

After Jonathan was born, the Lord graciously answered my prayer to be a stay-at-home mom. I absolutely loved spending time with my children, teaching and training them and watching them grow. Melissa had attended a private Christian school in California, but when we moved to North Carolina, were a family of five, living on a lower income and we could no longer afford private school. I pondered the idea of homeschooling, but not for long. I had known some people in California who homeschooled, and I thought I could never handle that. So, we decided to go the public school route instead.

Melissa attended a magnet middle school and was blessed to be in the gifted program. She was happy and thriving. Jonathan, on the other hand, was having a horrible experience in kindergarten. His very first day of school was a nightmare that still haunts me. I drove him to school that morning, but he wanted to ride the bus home with his big sister, so I agreed to let him have that school bus experience. When the bus arrived in front of our house that afternoon, Ellie and I were standing there with a plate of cupcakes, ready to hear all about his first day. Melissa got off the bus, alone. Looking distressed, she asked if I had already picked Jonathan up, because he wasn't on the bus. In a panic, I ran into the house and called the school! After what seemed like an eternity on hold, someone came on the line and told me that they had found him, on another bus in the city of Raleigh, which is also part of the Wake County School System. A driver arriving back at the school bus depot noticed one scared little boy still sitting in the back of the bus. They put him on the wrong bus at school and nobody had noticed! I put the girls in the van and literally sped to the bus depot, my mind filled with thoughts of my dark-haired, chubby-cheeked little "Beej," lost and terrified. I pulled into the lot, screeching on two wheels, jumped out of the van, and ran to find my son, sitting alone in an office, with tears streaming down his face. He was unharmed, but he never rode the bus again, and my confidence in the system began to wither.

After that, Jonathan would cry every morning when it was time to go to school. He already knew how to read and had always loved learning, but he hated school. He would come home with his lunch untouched, saying that he got a headache at school and couldn't eat. I watched in distress as he became more sad and withdrawn each day. I decided to become a room mother, so I could spend time in his classroom and see exactly what was troubling him. What I found was a typical kindergarten classroom, with twenty-seven children, the majority of whom were just learning their alphabet and how to hold scissors. Because he already knew how to read, the teacher had

Jonathan read books to the other children, which was fine, except he was bored because he was not learning anything new. The classroom was noisy and the teacher spent a lot of time dealing with disruptive behavior.

One day I was volunteering and couldn't wait to leave, because the chaos in the classroom had given me a terrible headache! As I sank into the seat of my car with a sigh of relief, I felt a stab in my heart. I had been able to leave, but my son didn't have that option! I was immediately convicted, and started to pray about what to do. Christmas break came and he was home for two delightful weeks. Jerry and I talked about finding a spot in a Christian school, but there were no openings in any nearby schools, and besides, we just couldn't afford it! The night before he was to go back to school, Jonathan fell apart, crying and telling me that he hated school and didn't want to go back. I started to cry too, and in my heart I knew that I needed to start homeschooling him. But I was terrified and felt that this was way more than I could handle!

As I took my fears and anxieties to the Lord, He began to open my eyes to the fact that I had been homeschooling my children ever since they were born! I had been the one to teach them to talk, to walk, to use the potty, to say please and thank you, to ride a bike, to play games, and even to read. So what was I afraid of? The Lord used Deuteronomy 6:5-9 and Matthew 22:37-40 to speak clearly to me.

Love the LORD your God with all your heart and with all your soul and with all your strength. These commandments that I give you today are to be upon your hearts. Impress them on your children. Talk about them when you sit at home and when you walk along the road, when you lie down and when you get up. Tie them as symbols on your hands and bind them on your foreheads. Write them on the doorframes of your houses and on your gates (Deuteronomy 6:5-9).

Jesus replied: "'Love the Lord your God with all your heart and with all your soul and with all your mind.' This is the first and greatest commandment. And the second is like it: 'Love your neighbor as yourself.' All the Law and the Prophets hang on these two commandments" (Matthew 22:37-40).

These verses showed me that God clearly wants all of us—

our heart, soul, and strength—to be fully devoted and committed to Him. He wants a personal relationship with us. He also gives us the responsibility of teaching our children about Him so they can have that relationship with Him too.

The family is the fundamental institution created by God for the nurturing and discipling of children. Parents have a great opportunity to influence our children as we spend our days together, sitting at home around the table, walking through the grocery aisles, lying on the bed for story time, and going about our day-to-day activities. Training and teaching our children in the ways of the Lord take a deliberate effort and lots of time—what we like to refer to today as quality time and quantity time. However, out of the 100 or so waking hours in a week, only 3 or 4 might be spent in church, while 30 or more are spent in school. During the hours outside of school, most children spend their time doing homework, participating in sports and organized activities, watching TV or playing video games. The time intentionally studying the Word of God is getting the short end of the stick.

When God graciously brought me out of the work force to be home with my children, He showed me that when I worked full-time outside the home, my job got the best part of me and my family got the leftovers. This had a negative impact on my marriage and my relationship with Melissa. He also showed me that sending my children off to school gets the best of them—their time, energy, even allegiance. How many times when you tell your child to do something they respond, "But my teacher said to do it this way!"? This just did not mesh with what I was learning from Scripture about the command and responsibility of parents and the purpose of families.

Needless to say, Jonathan never went back to school after Christmas break. We decided to homeschool because God radically transformed our understanding of our responsibility as parents. This is a calling, a priority and a conviction. *"... All authority in heaven and on earth has been given to me. Therefore go and make disciples of all nations, baptizing them in the name of the Father and of the Son and of the Holy Spirit, and teaching them to obey everything I have commanded you. And surely I am with you always, to the very end of the age" (Matthew 28:18-20).* I am called to intentionally and diligently disciple and teach my children all day and every day, passing along the baton of wisdom and faith to the next generation, so that they will come to know and place their trust in Jesus as their Lord and Savior. I often tell people, "If my child were to die today and find himself standing before God, is God going to ask him what grade he got on his SAT, or how to spell Constantinople? No, He is going to ask, *'Do you know Me? Do you love Me?'* So that has to be my primary focus." *My purpose is that they may be encouraged in heart and united in love, so that they may have the full riches of complete understanding, in order that they may know the mystery of God, namely, Christ, in whom are hidden all the treasures of wisdom and knowledge (Colossians 2:2-3). See to it that no one takes you captive through hollow and deceptive philosophy, which depends on human tradition and the basic principles of this world rather than on Christ (Colossians 2:8).*

Secondly, we work on character traits, behavior, manners, building relationships, handling conflict, communication and, of course, we learn math, grammar, history, and other subjects too. We read, create, sing, cook, play, clean, shop, garden, travel, and learn about God and His creation together as a family. Jerry and I intentionally look for the gifts and talents in our children so we can encourage and nurture them in those areas. We also focus on service and ministry. The children are very involved with our speaking ministry and with writing this book as well. We always have lots to talk and laugh about because we do so much life together.

Let me be clear. We are a family of sinners saved by grace, and we are far from perfect. God graciously allowed me to come home full-time, to teach my children and be the primary influence in their lives. I am grateful and take this responsibility very seriously, continually seeking His wisdom, and not the world's wisdom, in how to be the best educator I can. I read books, attend homeschool conferences, and belong to a local support group where I have found wonderful friends and mentors.

It is an honor and privilege to spend so much time with my children, and I really do love it. But it is also hard—sometimes really, REALLY hard! I get tired, grumpy, impatient, irritated, and frustrated. There are days when I feel like I just can't handle it all. I like my house to be clean and organized and chaos distresses me. It is stressful and requires a lot of organization and cooperation to juggle school work, prepare three meals plus snacks, do chores, laundry and housework all day long. Not to mention finding cuddle and play time, grocery shopping and all the other essentials of daily life. There are always more tasks to accomplish in a day than there are hours to do them. I pray constantly for the grace, patience and strength to accomplish what HE has for us each day and somehow it all works! When we come to the end of each day, we have memories and stories, and lots of laughter and love to share. The truth is, when we follow God's call on our lives, it usually requires doing hard things. Just look at Jesus' disciples and all they had to endure! Better yet, look at what Jesus had to endure! Nothing is harder than taking on the punishment for all the sins of the world. When I have those hard times and pity parties, I remind myself to take a deep breath, call on the Lord, and remember the truth of His Word and what really matters. I have no greater calling than to train up my children to know and to love the Lord. Too soon they will all be grown and gone, and I want them to have a happy and prosperous life in the Lord.

Our family has blossomed as a result of this choice. There have been struggles and challenges, and things haven't always gone as I planned, but we have also seen much positive fruit. Melissa had a unique situation because she stayed in the magnet school, but was very much a part of our homeschooling as well. We often signed her out of school to participate in whatever we were doing, including going to all the homeschool conferences and training seminars and traveling the country. She graduated from a magnet high school, and spent the next two years with YWAM (Youth with a Mission), serving God in England and Argentina. After that, she attended the University of the Nations in Hawaii, where she studied photography and design, and then went on to get her B.A. in Biblical Studies and History at the College at Southeastern Baptist Theological Seminary, Wake Forest, North Carolina. She is now married to Randy and they have three beautiful children. Melissa experienced both forms of education and said she plans to homeschool her own children.

She has taken a break from her photography business to be a full-time mom, and Randy is in the process of becoming a restaurant owner-operator. We are so proud of the family they have become and cherish every moment we have with them.

Jonathan was the first graduate of our homeschool, Mestas Christian Academy. Through dual enrollment at the local community college, he was able to start pursuing a career as a firefighter while still in high school. He was a volunteer Junior Firefighter for two years, and became the youngest man accepted into the Firefighter Training Academy. He then served four years as a full-time Firefighter. In 2011, he was granted a leave of absence to serve with YWAM Ozarks in Asia. He recently felt led to resign from his career as a firefighter and return to YWAM to serve on staff for the next six months. He has also enlisted in the United States Army and starts Airborne Ranger School in 2013. He is beginning the exciting next chapter of his faith journey in life.

Ellie has traveled on missions trips to specifically serve in orphanages in China, Guatemala, Ethiopia, and Uganda, and at age fifteen, started her own orphan care ministry. She organized and led a team to serve in orphanages and the community in Uganda in 2010. While in high school she became a certified Doula and Child Birth Educator, and graduated in 2011. She is currently in nursing school studying to be a Certified Nurse Midwife. Because she saw that many children are orphaned because of poor medical and prenatal care, she had the desire to learn a skill that is beneficial in serving women and children.

Just when I thought Mestas Christian Academy was coming to a close, the Lord sent me five more precious children to start training all over again. I am currently teaching the twinettes kindergarten, the twins second grade and the man in the middle first grade. By the time they all graduate, I will have homeschooled for thirty-four years, and I will be sixty-five years old. That is, if the Lord wills me to live that long.

I know, that I know, God has called me for such a time as this, and He is faithful to give me the grace, strength, and resources to accomplish His will. I am still learning new things every day. I know how fast children grow up, and I want to cherish every day I have with them. Too soon, they will be flying the nest on their own journey of faith. I am grateful for the close family relationships we have, and the great treasure chest of memories we are building together. Our house is loud, crowded, and full of craziness that can sometimes be overwhelming, but it is a house full of faith, joy, laughter, and lots of luv, luv, luv!

I have no greater joy than to hear that my children are walking in the truth (3 John 4).

3 Do You Really Love Me?

"... Simon son of John, do you truly love me more than these?" "Yes, Lord," he said, "you know that I love you." Jesus said, "Feed my lambs." Again Jesus said, "Simon son of John, do you truly love me?" He answered, "Yes, Lord, you know that I love you." Jesus said, "Take care of my sheep." The third time he said to him, "Simon son of John, do you love me?" Peter was hurt because Jesus asked him the third time, "Do you love me?" He said, "Lord, you know all things; you know that I love you." Jesus said, "Feed my sheep. I tell you the truth, when you were younger you dressed yourself and went where you wanted; but when you are old you will stretch out your hands, and someone else will dress you and lead you where you do not want to go." Jesus said this to indicate the kind of death by which Peter would glorify God. Then he said to him, "FOLLOW ME!" (John 21:15-19, emphasis added).

While attending a homeschool conference, I was convicted by this passage. I had to ask myself if my life was truly representing that I loved Jesus. Am I feeding His sheep, and willing to die a death that would glorify God? Am I following Him wholeheartedly? Do I really love Him? This passage showed me that I am to live my life with arms wide open, giving all control to God, even being willing to die on a cross. That means giving up my agenda and living for His. I asked God to show me how I could be more in love with Him and give Him all of me. I knew I needed to repent and surrender more of my life to Him. When I went home and shared this with Jerry, we both agreed that there was one area of our lives that we still felt guilty about, and we had not done everything to give control back to God. It was the control of our family. We believed God did have another son for us as He whispered to my heart. We were willing and even prayed to receive more children and hoped the vasectomy didn't work, but deep down we knew we needed to take the physical steps to surrender total control of this area of our lives back to God.

We can say we love and trust Him, but in reality, there are many areas of our lives that we hold with a clenched fist, instead of holding our arms wide open. This was one area that we knew was a problem for us. This was at the top of our heap. As I study the Scriptures, every time it refers to children it is always in the context of a "gift" and "blessing" from the Lord, and my heart would ache. We had decided to tell God, "No more gifts or blessings for us, please, we don't want any more." Our conviction was deep and painful.

You foolish man, do you want evidence that faith without deeds is useless? Was not our ancestor Abraham considered righteous for what he did when he offered his son Isaac on the altar? You see that his faith and his actions were working together, and his faith was made complete by what he did. And the scripture was fulfilled that says, "Abraham believed God, and it was credited to him as righteousness," and he was called God's friend. You see that a person is justified by what he does and not by faith alone (James 2:20-24).

It was time to take action and get a vasectomy reversal. When we had the vasectomy, it was covered by insurance and there were many doctors to choose from. We were surprised to find that a reversal is completely different. It costs between $10,000 and $15,000 and was not covered by insurance. There was only one doctor in Chapel Hill that performed this procedure. Isn't it true that to fall into sin and disobedience is always easy and to get out is always harder? We did not have the money, so we started to pray and ask for a miracle.

One day at a homeschool co-op class, I was talking with my friend Casey and she shared that her husband just had a vasectomy reversal. She said they were convicted they were not trusting God for their family. I was shocked that she was sharing this with me, because I had never told anyone about our situation. I asked her where he had the surgery, and she told me about Dr. Stanton in Conway, Arkansas who does this surgery as a ministry. He is a vascular surgeon who was called by God to study this particular procedure and to perform this surgery as a ministry to His people. He only charged $1,000 to cover his costs. She gave me his telephone number, and when I shared it with Jerry, we called the doctor immediately.

Dr. Stanton explained that he must interview Jerry first, because he only took certain people into his ministry. When Jerry shared his testimony, the doctor said this was exactly why God told him to start this ministry. It is for HIS people that are being called into the awakening to His plan for growing their families. He also said he only did his ministry surgery on Friday. Jerry and I were ecstatic! We knew this was a divine answer to our prayers and began the plan to save money and get him there. We unexpectedly received a check from a class action lawsuit at Jerry's job for $624, then received an overpayment refund for $47, and had a yard sale and scraped up $300 toward our goal. The money just started coming in.

Then Jerry got a call from an elder at our church inviting him to go with a team of men to Little Rock, Arkansas. They were going to meet with Dennis Rainey of *FamilyLife Today*® and discuss opportunities for future ministry at our church. The elder said all expenses would be paid and they would be there from Friday through Sunday. We immediately knew this was God's provision to get Jerry to Arkansas. There was a problem, though; the doctor said he only performed surgery on Friday and this schedule wasn't going to work. We called the doctor and explained the situation and the dates Jerry would be there. To our amazement, he agreed to perform the surgery on Monday, after the conference. We were in awe of His divine provision.

Conway was at least an hour from Little Rock, so the plan was that Jerry would rent a car and drive to Conway after the conference. It also turned out that he had accumulated enough points through his job to get two free hotel nights. The Lord was providing everything we needed. Jerry shared this testimony with the elders of our church, and they agreed to make his return flight later than the rest of the team. He also shared with the men at the conference and it was a testimony to every man on the team. Sunday morning they attended church with Dennis Rainey and then prayed for a successful surgery as they parted ways.

Jerry went to the counter at the church lobby and asked for a telephone book to get a rental car to drive to Conway. The person at the desk told him to wait just a minute. She came back with a young couple that attended the church, who just happened to be driving to Conway that day to visit family, offering to give him a ride. They took him to the hotel that just happened to be a few blocks from the doctor's office. Jerry called and told me about this latest miracle of provision. What were the odds of that happening? I asked if he'd remembered to request a room near the ice machine, since he was going to need lots of it after the surgery. I felt so badly that I could not go with him, but we had no one to care for our kids and no money to pay the extra plane fare. He said he had forgotten, but to hold on while he checked the hall. He came back and said, "Eileen, can you believe the ice machine is right outside my door?"

The clerk at hotel check-in had told him they had a shuttle that would take him to the doctor, in the morning, for free. When Jerry went for the surgery, the doctor shared his testimony about how he too was convicted to trust God for his family. He had just had his eighth child and one of his older sons was his assistant during the surgery. Then he had his son drive Jerry back to the hotel and got him settled in. It was absolutely amazing. Jerry was surprised that even the recovery from this surgery was not as painful as the initial vasectomy. He was up and walking by the next day, and came home a new man.

The doctor said he thought we had an 80% chance of getting pregnant, because everything looked good during the surgery. We were excited about the possibility of our family growing again, but more importantly, we felt like we were back in obedience to the Lord. We were putting our trust in Him and asking for His blessing.

We were hopeful that we would soon be pregnant after all the Lord had done for this provision. We were praying specifically for "Jeremiah" to come. It was time to wait and trust again.

I began to realize there are a lot of areas of my life where I have control, and I want to clean out the closet, so to speak, and give it all back to Him. I want to get to the place where I trust God in all things and allow Him to show me what He wants to do. This will be a lifelong journey, but it starts with listening to His voice, and then being willing to step out in faith to see what He has planned. This was another situation that proved to be more than we could handle, but the Lord proved faithful.

4 Journey to Jeremiah James

*Do not merely listen to the word, and so deceive yourselves.
Do what it says (James 1:22).*

*Religion that God our Father accepts as pure and faultless is
this: to look after orphans and widows in their distress and to keep
oneself from being polluted by the world (James 1:27).*

A year passed and we were still waiting and praying for
Jeremiah. A spirit of restlessness started to happen in our home
again. Since we were not getting pregnant, we began to wonder if
God wanted us to adopt him. As the Lord would have it, within
weeks, while at church, Pastor Jeff Doyle was teaching from the
book of James. I sat, listening intently, and knew God was speaking
directly to me. I began to cry and when I looked over at Jerry, he was
crying too. When we got home, I was very quiet and waited a few
hours before asking him why he had cried. I was nervous because I
knew we were about to embark on another journey from the Lord.
We shared what the Lord had convicted us of and it was the same
message for both of us.

The Lord was telling us to start the adoption process. As we
agreed the Lord was telling us to again take action, I felt impressed
that we were to name our son Jeremiah James, because the Lord
used these two verses to communicate He was sending a son to us.
Jeremiah 29:11-14: He knows the plans He has for us, He knows
how many children and when, how and where He is sending them
from. James 1:22 and 27 told us we were responsible to care for
orphans in their distress and to start the adoption process. It was time

to get busy and stop waiting. So, we began the journey to Jeremiah James through adoption.

Ever since I was very young, I had a desire to adopt a child. I was raised in a generation that believed adoption was only for people who could not have children. It was Plan B. I didn't know a single person who was adopted until I was an adult. It was also common practice to keep it a secret, as if it was something to be ashamed of. In my world, adoption was foreign. Because I had biological children, I knew how much I loved them and loved being a mom. I wanted to adopt, but I did wonder if I would love this child as much. In the back of my mind, I was afraid. I didn't want to treat this child differently. I prayed God would give me the same kind of love, and I had no idea what to expect. This was another step of faith.

When we told the kids we were going to start the process, Melissa still thought we were too old. She was now graduated and on her way to serve with YWAM. Jonathan said he wanted a real brother to come from my womb, but our sweet Ellie was absolutely elated. She would get so excited when an information packet would arrive from an adoption agency. She started to read all the information and watch the enclosed videos on her own. She would watch them every day, as they became her favorite programs.

As the journey began, we were discouraged by the costs. We felt led to a domestic adoption and we did not have $15,000-plus in the bank. We prayed and asked God to show us how to proceed. We knew He was calling us to do this and needed to trust Him for provision again. I heard on the radio one morning that there was a new program for children to be adopted out of the foster care system at no cost. So we made an appointment to attend a seminar at the Social Services Department of Wake County.

We sat through half of the seminar and came to the conclusion that foster care was not going to work for us. We were very discouraged and decided to leave. As we were walking down the hall, someone mentioned that the meeting for adoption was in another room. Even though it was half over, we asked if we could join them. We were surprised to find that the meeting was being conducted by the Children's Home Society Adoption Agency. When I asked what the fees were, the caseworker, Brenda, said there was no charge to the adoptive family. We immediately perked up and signed up for a home visit. And this began our first journey to adoption.

About two weeks later, Brenda Farnsworth, our caseworker from Children's Home Society of North Carolina, was sitting at our kitchen table. She interviewed all of us and then asked what our preferences were for adoption. She wrote it on a piece of paper as I spoke. I told her, "God already told us we are getting a baby boy, and we have been praying for him for several years now. His name is Jeremiah James. We prefer him to be biracial Hispanic/White like our biological children, but we will take whatever God sends us. We prefer a healthy, drug free baby, less than two years old. And if possible, we would love to get twins, because we don't want him to be like an only child." Ellie was already nine years old, and we thought we would probably start another adoption soon after this one, so that we wouldn't have a lonely little boy.

Brenda picked up the piece of paper she had written on, handed it to me and said, "Rip it up. You will never get what you just asked for." I was so surprised. She said, "I have worked many years in this area and Hispanic children are rarely released for adoption. They usually go to a family member. Twins are definitely a rarity and healthy is very unlikely. Most of the children that get placed are due to health or drug and abuse issues. So, if you still want to proceed with this adoption you need to be willing to take whatever is available." I looked at her very seriously and said, "Brenda, I know this is weird, but God already told us we are getting a baby boy. I don't know all the details for sure, but I have learned to never put God in a box. He can do all things!" With that, we agreed to proceed with the paperwork.

We spent the next eight months praying for Jeremiah James, and specifically, for twins. There were several times when we would forget to specify the twin part and Ellie would get so upset. One night she pounded her fist on the table because we had forgotten several times in a row. I looked at her and said, "Ellie, since you are so adamant about the twins, if God gives them to us, we will all know that is His answer to your specific prayer." We all really wanted to have twins.

On July 6, 2003 we arrived home at approximately 11:00 p.m. from Jonathan's baseball tournament. When we checked our voicemail there was a message from the adoption agency saying to call them immediately, no matter what time we got home. We called and got Brenda's supervisor Debra, since Brenda was on vacation. She told us, "You have been selected to be the parents of full Hispanic twin baby boys! They are twenty-seven week preemies, currently in the Neonatal Intensive Care Unit at New Hanover Hospital in Wilmington, North Carolina. They weighed in at 1.9 pounds and 2.3 pounds at birth." I was in shock and began to cry. Everyone was standing by the phone and could hear the news. We all began to jump for joy and then she said, "Wait, there is more. Baby 'B' had a brain bleed at birth. Bleeds run in range from 1-5, and he had a grade 3. This means he most likely has cerebral palsy and other serious health issues. Due to their prematurity they may also be blind, deaf, and have severe learning disabilities. They have chronic lung disease and we really won't know the true extent of all of their issues until they get older. They have been in the hospital for seven weeks and are getting ready to be released. We will need you to be there in twenty-four hours, if you decide to take them. I will give you until tomorrow by 11:00 a.m. to call me back with your answer."

Without any hesitation, we all looked at each other in agreement as I said, "Debra, we have been praying for three years now for Jeremiah James Mestas. We don't need any more time to decide. God has given us **JEREMIAH AND JAMES!!** We will be their parents." We all started to scream and cry and jump for joy. We could not believe this was really happening. In fact, we had been so unsure of what was going to happen since our first meeting with Brenda, that we didn't even tell anyone we were in the adoption process. Then we realized we only had twenty-four hours to get ready for newborn twins! We ran up to the attic and started to pull down the crib and baby supplies. We stayed up all night planning what had to be done. We called our friends and made arrangements for the kids to stay with them. Everyone started to call our church members and spread the good news. We called my mom and dad and told them the news. They were shocked and wanted to know why we would adopt children with severe health issues. They did not think this was a good idea. This was not what we ideally wanted and I was concerned that we were going to incur large medical bills. But I knew in my heart that it was an opportunity to trust and obey God.

We called Melissa, who was living in Hawaii, attending the University of the Nations with YWAM (Youth with a Mission). We woke her in the middle of the night and told her we had some very special news. "We are getting twin baby boys tomorrow!" She screamed, "What, are you crazy? You guys are too old! How can this be happening?" We told her all the details, and she too was shocked by what we were about to take on. She was sad that she couldn't be here for their arrival, but she was scheduled to come home a month later. Poor kid, she just never knew what to expect from her mom and dad. She immediately remembered that family meeting we had when she was a senior in high school, when I shared how the Lord told us He was sending us a son. Jeremiah James had arrived! When she got home and saw the twins for the first time, she said they looked like two little monkeys. They were so tiny, wrinkled and fragile, and still looked like newborns. But she was so happy to be their big sister, and joined the team of caretakers, loving on them constantly.

This three-year faith journey of waiting for Jeremiah James prepared me to honestly believe this was my assignment from the Lord. I realized that a normal pregnancy was forty weeks and these guys were born at twenty-seven. They were only half-cooked, which made me think there were definitely going to be some issues. While having handicapped children was not my first choice, I was ready to accept this task and prayed for the Lord to equip us to handle it. We were already talking about learning sign language and Braille and whatever else was necessary to care for our precious baby boys. I could picture myself pushing a wheelchair and having these boys for the rest of my life. God never makes mistakes. He never has to say, *"Oh, no, how did that one slip by Me? I didn't see that one."* No, all things happen with God's divine plan and purpose. In the back of my mind, I did wonder if I was going to be able to handle it well; would this be too much for me? We managed to get everything in order and drove two hours to the hospital.

During our waiting process, I had also been praying that if the Lord was sending us a newborn baby, He would give me the miracle of breast-feeding, like I did my biological children. I had heard stories of other adoptive moms who were able to do this. I am a very strong advocate of breast-feeding and wanted to be able to bond with my new baby and give the best nutrition possible. I knew this was going to take a miracle, because my Ellie was now ten years old, and I stopped nursing her when she was two.

When Jonathan was born, I became a huge advocate for breast-feeding. I was carting him all over town while Melissa attended school, ballet, etc. and I was concerned about maintaining his schedule and my modesty while in public. The Lord gave me a dream to design a nursing cover so I could accomplish these goals. We called it the "Can't–a–Peek™ Nursing Canopy." I was blessed to have my design patented and started a manufacturing company to produce them for mass distribution. We were featured in the *One Step Ahead* catalog for many years, as well as in individual baby stores in the USA and Canada. This was our family business for twelve years. As the manufacturing industry moved overseas, we had to make a choice to go to China, Mexico or shut it down. We decided it was time to close up shop. My design is still being manufactured by other companies today, and I am blessed every time I see one in public. When I nursed my older children, I always had a great supply and nursed a total of five years of my life.

So when I got to the hospital and I saw these tiny little boys hooked up to machines, my heart just ached. I knew they needed breast milk to help them thrive. I immediately asked the nurse to get me a breast pump. She looked at me with surprise and asked if I had another nursing baby at home. I told her ten years ago I did, and she just looked at me like I was joking or crazy. When I told her I was as serious as a heart attack, the other nurse in the room went to get one. She literally came running into the room with the pump. I sat down and hooked it up while Jerry was holding the babies. I prayed, "Dear Lord, you know what these boys need, and I am asking for this miracle, please." To the amazement of us all, within fifteen minutes I had a letdown and my milk was in! I let out a sigh of gratitude, as I burst into tears at the blessing from the Lord. Other nurses were soon coming in to see me as the word was spreading throughout the unit. Many left in tears and awe. I never got a huge milk supply to sustain them full-time, but I had enough for their appetizer three times a day. I was able to breast-feed the boys for the first three months of their lives. This was another miracle from the Lord!

We spent four days in the hospital learning how to care for the twins. It was like I had just given birth to them. We slept in the room and tended to their every need. I gave them both a bath within minutes of arriving. We even got "stork bucks" to have dinner in the cafeteria, just like biological parents. I joked that I was feeling great for just having twins. We got a crash course in being a neonatal nurse. We had to operate the pulse oximeters, breathing machines, learn their feeding schedule, weigh and chart their progress, and be taught how to revive them when the boys stopped breathing.

Dr. McArtor had been their pediatrician since birth and he was very protective over them. In fact, when he came in the room and met us, he was surprised that they were being adopted. He had met their birth parents and said that they were so loving toward the boys, he had no idea that they were going to put them up for adoption. The parents decided to give them up because they were not able to provide the medical care the children needed. The doctor agreed the travel back to Mexico could have been fatal.

Dr. McArtor was in love with these boys. He had spent many hours holding and caring for them for seven weeks. He was the one who insisted that we had to stay with them for four days to understand the magnitude of caring for them, before we could take them home. He wanted to be sure we knew what we were getting into. On our last day there, he came to give us a big hug and thank us for what we were doing.

I hugged him so tight and thanked him for all he had done to save their lives. He had explained every detail of their birth and treatment, and said there were a few times he didn't know if they would survive. He was hopeful that they would not have too many health issues, but agreed that only time would reveal them. Again, there were many tears!

Driving home from the hospital, we got on Highway 40 right where it begins. This highway runs straight across the United States and ends in Los Angeles, California. There is a sign that says, Los Angeles, California—2,400 miles. When I saw that, I instantly heard a whisper, *This is one of the reasons I brought you to North Carolina. Your babies were born here and this was all part of My plan.*

When we arrived at home, there were balloons and a crowd to

welcome us. The front porch was full of baby supplies, diapers, baby swings, walkers, clothes, etc. Several friends, and especially Angela Kinsley, had gotten the news while we were gone, and started to bring supplies to the house. It was a blessing to see God's people pouring out love and support to our family.

We spent the next six months quarantined to our house except for doctors' appointments. The boys were very fragile and we could not have visitors either. They had chronic lung disease, which meant a common cold could kill them. We set up the living room like a hospital room and I slept on the couch. Our lives unexpectedly took a drastic change within a week. The boys had to be fed every two hours around the clock, and that included breast-feeding them. Needless to say, I didn't get much sleep or do anything else, for that matter.

Jonathan was thirteen years old and Ellie ten years old. Our school became "Preemie Neonatal Care 101." Every day I had plans to do school, but it just never happened. They took care of the chores in the house, took turns feeding and charting the babies' progress, worked the machines, measured bottles and formula, and held the boys all day long. We wanted them to be held as much as possible. They were so tiny that they fit into the pocket on Ellie's blanket, which was the size of an average book.

The goal was to have them gaining weight every week, so we had to watch the clock faithfully for feedings. They also had GERD (Gastro Esophageal Reflux Disease), which meant they threw up constantly. So many times we would just finish a feeding, they would throw it all up, and we would have to feed them again. It was crazy!

We were in a special Neonatal Care program at Wake Med Hospital in Raleigh, where we had to see specialists every week. We were being sent to Duke Hospital and all over town. They were looking for all the suspected health issues, to begin immediate intervention. With each visit, they would do testing, evaluations, write reports and tell us to come back next month. When we went for the boys' twelve-month check-up, the doctor came into the room with two huge files in his arms. He put them on the counter and looked at me with a very serious look on his face. He folded his arms and said, "Mrs. Mestas, I don't know what it is you have, but I want some of it." He leaned over and rubbed his elbow on mine and said, "These are the remarkable miracle boys! I have been a NIC unit doctor for twenty years and I have never seen this. We can find absolutely nothing wrong with these boys. Everything has come back normal. In fact, there is absolutely no residue from the brain bleed on the CT scan, which is miraculous. A grade 3 level will usually leave a scar. I am just amazed because they had all odds against them. First, they were twenty-seven week preemies, and that alone is cause for health issues. Being twins added additional risks. I am just amazed!" Mom, Ellie and I began to cry and I said, "Yes, Doctor, these are remarkable miracle boys. This is the will of God for their lives, and even if they did have serious health issues, they would still be miracles. God never makes mistakes and children with health issues are just as miraculous."

He added that he was sure that the love and nurturing care we had been giving them also played a role in their progress. He said if we had not adopted them, they probably would not have survived. Then he added, "I am going home tonight to talk to my wife about adoption. I have been so moved by working with your family." With tears in his eyes, he said, "Thank you."

When we began this adoption, we were concerned about all the medical costs. We knew our insurance would not pay for all of it and we thought we were going to accumulate a lot of medical bill debt. After we agreed to take this on and signed all the papers, we were informed that the twins had 100% medical coverage through Medicaid until the age of eighteen. The Lord provided!

As if we hadn't experienced enough, the Lord provided another miracle. The first year we got the boys, we were so busy taking care of them that we didn't crack one school book. This was the first time in my homeschool career that we did not do school on a daily basis. One day I realized it was time for annual testing. The homeschool law in North Carolina requires all students to be tested by a certified representative. I told Jerry that Jonathan and Ellie were probably going to fail the Iowa Aptitude test, and I was afraid our homeschool was going to be shut down. We prayed before their exams, reminding the Lord we'd had no time to do school because of all the work to care for these babies. I just had to surrender to Him and trust that He was in control. The test results came back a month later. We all stood around the kitchen, as I opened them with shaking hands and fear. To our amazement, both Jonathan and Ellie scored two grade levels higher across the board. Even their math skills improved and we hadn't cracked the math book all year. With sobbing tears again, I realized this was another lesson from the Lord, teaching us when we are in His will, we have nothing to fear. He is in the business of equipping us all to be about His business and to accomplish His plans. He is Jehovah Jireh, the Great Provider, and worthy to be praised!

Comments from Brenda Farnsworth, our caseworker with the Children's Home Society of North Carolina adoption agency:

First and foremost, I was privileged to meet the Mestas family. Love and faith radiated from them. I could tell it was a 'calling' for them and I wanted to do everything I could to help find 'their children.' Their strong faith was such an inspiration to me, and still is. When I first met them, I thought it would be impossible to meet their expectations ... but I believed in them and their vision. I was overwhelmed with the miracle that occurred when the birth parents for James and Jeremiah chose Jerry and Eileen's family. These children were MEANT to be with them. Eileen and Jerry went the extra mile to help these fragile babies thrive ... and thrive they did. With every visit I made I could see how much progress they were making. The whole Mestas family rallied around and helped out, surrounding the children with loving care. I have no doubt they have instilled a strong faith in their children—their many children! Eileen and Jerry are a blessing, as are their children. God works in mysterious ways, and He knew what He was doing when Eileen and Jerry were selected for their precious boys, and the others that soon followed.

5 A Full Quiver and No Job

" 'Our Father in heaven, hallowed be your name, your kingdom come, your will be done on earth as it is in heaven. Give us today our daily bread. Forgive us our debts, as we also have forgiven our debtors, And lead us not into temptation, but deliver us from the evil one' " (Matthew 6:9-13).

There's never a dull moment in our house. The twins were just over a year old, and their health was improving every day. Psalm 127:4-5 (NASB) says, *Like arrows in the hand of a warrior, So are the children of one's youth. How blessed is the man whose quiver is full of them.* Well, our quiver was now full of five children and we were happy. We renovated our walk-out basement into an apartment, and my parents came up from Florida and moved in with us. Jerry was working as a fraud investigator and life was good. Then suddenly, he lost his job.

Jerry went to work that Friday morning like every other day, to investigate a possible fraudulent insurance claim. In the course of an investigation, he often had to interview people at their workplace. That day, he was assigned to interview a woman during her lunch break at a women's medical clinic. As he finished the interview and was getting ready to leave, he noticed that the atmosphere in the place was very somber and quiet. He heard a man at the desk ask how long before his wife would be finished. As Jerry walked to his car, he saw that same man walking to his car as well.

As Jerry was backing out of the parking space to leave, he suddenly had a strong feeling that he needed to go talk to that man, who was sitting in the car a few spots down. He hesitated, mumbling to himself that he was in a hurry and didn't have time. As soon as he said it, he knew he was being disobedient, and this was the Lord talking to him! So Jerry pulled back into the parking spot and walked over to the car, where the man was sitting with his window open.

Noticing that the man was crying and very distraught, Jerry gently asked if he was okay and if he needed help. The man looked up with tears in his eyes, sharing that he and his wife had been married for several years, but were now headed for divorce. She had gotten pregnant and was in the clinic right now to get an abortion. An abortion clinic! Jerry had no idea. Feeling a deep sense of compassion for the man and his situation, he asked the man if he was a Christian. When he said yes, Jerry reminded him of what the Bible teaches about human life, and told the man to go get his wife. Jerry even showed him the photo of our newly adopted twins and offered to adopt their baby, if he would just get her out of there. Jerry told him God had a plan for this child and there were other options. They prayed together, the man seemed to calm down, and agreed that he was going to go back inside and talk to his wife.

Jerry walked back to his car and started to back out of his parking space again, when suddenly, the man was standing at the car window with a piece of paper in his hand. The man handed Jerry the paper with his wife's name written on it. He was shaking, and asked Jerry to go into the clinic for him and ask that his wife come out to talk with him. Jerry's immediate response was, "No, you need to go in there and get your wife!" But the man began to cry and said he just couldn't. He was very agitated. Jerry felt sorry for him, so he agreed to go inside. Jerry handed the paper to the receptionist and said, "This woman's husband is outside and he is very upset. He needs her to go out and talk to him." With that, Jerry left, got in his car and drove to the other side of the parking lot to see what was going to happen. He called me, told me all that had happened, and then watched the wife come out of the clinic and stand at the car window, talking with her husband. He told me she was obviously pregnant and that we really needed to pray for them.

I started to cry so hard that I couldn't pray, so Jonathan took over. Jonathan, Ellie and I were literally on the floor, pleading with the Lord on behalf of this couple we had never met and their unborn child. Ellie and I were crying and Jonathan began to pray, "Lord, please be with this couple and give them courage to leave. Help them with their marriage and help them not to abort their baby." Within a minute of his prayer, Jerry called back to tell us that the wife had gotten in the car and they had driven away! We all rejoiced, with tears of joy this time, and felt like God had just given us a divine appointment to pray for this couple.

At church two days later, Jerry shared this story and our whole congregation prayed for that couple. What we didn't know was just how much this divine appointment was going to change our lives and the lives of our church. We were about to begin another faith journey that would radically impact us all.

When Jerry went to work the next week, his boss told him to report to the Human Resources department. When he arrived, he was told that he was being fired for inappropriate conduct. The clinic had filed a report that Jerry had caused them to lose business. He had to immediately turn in his company car and was allowed to make a quick phone call in front of them, just to get a ride home. He was treated like a criminal!

As you can imagine, this came as a great shock to us all! After we absorbed what had happened, I remember thinking, "Wait. This is going to turn out great. God obviously put you in that clinic by divine appointment and He orchestrated all of this to happen. I'll bet this means He has an even better job for you. We don't have to worry! Everything is going to be just fine." We started to call our friends and ask them to pray for the new job that we just knew was around the corner. Our church family was a vital part of our lives, and all of us together eagerly awaited another miracle.

That doesn't mean we didn't face anxiety and even fear. Because of the circumstances surrounding his termination, Jerry didn't qualify for unemployment. Here we were with five children, including our infant twin boys, which meant buying diapers and formula for two. My parents had just moved in and were depending on us for a roof over their heads as well. We suddenly had no job or unemployment benefits, no medical insurance, and very little savings. We had Jerry's pension check from LAPD and the stipend payments for the boys from the state adoption program, but it wasn't enough to cover all the expenses. Jerry was sending out resumes, but for the first time in his life he could not get a job.

After several months, we made a list of all his skills and talents and he started his own company, Mestas & Associates. He got his Private Investigator's license renewed and started to promote his Spanish interpreter's expertise. Two friends who have their own business had a need for his Spanish skills, so every morning Jerry woke up and would juggle whichever job had work that day. Some days and weeks there was no work at all.

In the midst of this trial, we started to see God's people step into our lives and live out the gospel in amazing ways. We came home to find groceries on our front porch, gift cards in the mail and cards and e-mails of encouragement. One day I came home to find $1,500 cash in an envelope on my door. Family and friends started sending us money to help out too. People we knew, in difficult financial situations themselves, were sending us money. We always got exactly what we needed for that month's bills and not a penny more. During this time, Jerry submitted an article to *Focus on the Family Citizen®* magazine, sharing his testimony, and it was published. As a result, people we didn't even know started to send notes of encouragement and support. One lady in Texas sent a box of homemade doll clothes with matching dresses for Ellie. She wrote and told us she had no money, but that God had given her the talent to sew. She wanted to be sure we had a gift for Ellie to put under the Christmas tree that year.

One morning I was praying for a $1,000 payment that was due within the week. I was shocked to find an envelope stuck to my door that afternoon with exactly $1,000 cash inside. There was a beautiful note of encouragement, saying the Lord had prompted these friends to give it to us. I ran into the kitchen, crying and thanking God for this provision. And then I heard Him whisper, *"Take half of the money to Mary right now. Her husband is out of work too."* I honestly looked up and said, "Lord, but You know we need this." I was immediately convicted and heard Him say, *"Trust Me!"* I was ashamed of my selfishness, but I was grateful that the LORD was teaching me to give sacrificially as well. I grabbed my keys and drove right to Mary's house.

Mary and Michael Moore have been friends of ours for sixteen years. About ten years ago, we even had an official adoption ceremony with homemade certificates declaring we are family. Their children call us aunt and uncle. When I told her what had happened and handed her the money, she too was in tears. She had been praying that morning to meet a bill of $500 that was due that very day. We were both blessed to know the Lord was hearing our prayers and teaching us to trust Him. Of course, the rest of the money came in to make our bills that week. To this day, I thank God for that lesson.

God used this time to teach me that our security and our provision come from Him and not my husband's job. For the first time in our marriage, we were unemployed. We were humbled that God was using this time to strip us of our pride and false belief that we were in control of our provisions. He alone is in control of it all. We watched Him intentionally move the hearts of others to sacrificially give to us. We were getting food from the food bank at church, from friends, and friends of friends that we didn't know. People were delivering cooked meals and bringing groceries. When I told Ellie's piano teacher that she had to quit lessons because we didn't have the money to pay for it, he said that Ellie could stay as his student for as long as she wanted. We were amazed as we watched God move His people and bring attention to what He had done.

Jerry did file an appeal with the State Board of Unemployment, because he knew he had done nothing wrong. The process took a year and he acted as his own attorney. To the glory of the Lord, he won his case and we were reimbursed for all of the unemployment payments he was originally denied. Still, we had no idea that for two years, three months, and eleven days we would be on this journey of faith. We learned how to pray for our daily bread like never before. We found ourselves in another season of going deeper into a trust and love relationship with the Lord, and with every trial we learned to SEE and HEAR Him ever more clearly.

6 The Wedding

"Hallelujah! For our Lord God Almighty reigns. Let us rejoice and be glad and give him glory! For the wedding of the Lamb has come, and his bride has made herself ready. Fine linen, bright and clean, was given her to wear. ... "'Blessed are those who are invited to the wedding supper of the Lamb!'" (Revelation 19:6-9).

By this time, Melissa had returned from photography school in Hawaii and was a student at The College at Southeastern right here in our town, living at home while getting her degree in Biblical Studies and History. She also worked as a photographer with a prominent wedding studio in Raleigh, which helped pay for her school expenses. As the Lord would have it, she soon met Randy, the man of her dreams, and after several months it became apparent that they were meant for each other. Randy asked for her hand in marriage and the wedding bells started ringing.

Weddings are a very big deal in both Jerry's and my families, with the expectation of a big party, complete with dinner and dancing at the wedding reception. We both come from large families—Jerry is one of thirteen kids!—we knew this could get expensive, and we were feeling the pressure. How were we going to pay for a beautiful wedding for our first-born daughter, when we were unemployed? We were feeling like failures. Even Ellie said, "Mama, why would God bring Sissy's husband now, when Papa is out of work and you have no money to pay for her wedding?" I could only respond, "I don't know, Ellie, but I know He is in control of everything. Maybe He is going to teach us another lesson that we don't have to have the wedding we want."

Melissa had been the photographer at some really beautiful and expensive weddings, and she would come home and tell me about all the things she would like to have at her wedding someday. She didn't want extravagance, but she started planning what her dream wedding would look like. She especially talked about having beautiful flower arrangements.

We never dreamed her wedding day would come during our financial crisis. We realized it was just going to have to be different than what we had dreamed. Instead of a big, elaborate party, we would have a small gathering of family and friends and just serve cake. I was going to make it and we knew everyone would understand. Through a friend's company, we were able to get beautiful invitations at cost. I had a gold ring with rubies that I sold at a consignment jewelry store and got enough money to buy her dress. We were scraping things together, and then we got the surprise we never expected.

Melissa went to the regularly scheduled staff meeting at work. They were discussing their upcoming wedding schedule, when the wedding coordinator asked her why she hadn't talked to them about her wedding yet. Melissa explained that her dad was still out of work and we were not able to give her a big wedding reception. She knew their prices and we could not afford to hire any of them. As she sat there in humility, explaining that she was perfectly content and didn't need a big wedding, they politely interrupted her. "Melissa, we have talked about it and want to put on the wedding for free. We are family here!" She almost fell over and burst into tears. She had no idea they were waiting to hear from her so they could start planning her wedding for free!

On a beautiful November evening in 2006, the Lord gave Melissa the wedding of her dreams, in spite of our situation. She had a wedding coordinator, professional photographers, professional florist, DJ and videographer. We were able to scrape up the money to rent a lovely banquet room, and a friend of mine who owns a catering company helped us with a dessert and coffee banquet. The flower arrangements were the most beautiful ones I have ever seen. Relatives came from across the country and we were able to take them to dinner at our favorite Italian restaurant. It was a glorious day!

Again, we learned another lesson of trust. We made sure

everyone knew how the Lord miraculously provided for this wedding, down to the smallest details, and everyone was in awe. Adults and children alike knew they were part of something very special. It was absolutely amazing to SEE the Lord stir the hearts of so many people to provide a wedding banquet fit for a princess—the daughter of the King!

7 China Adoption

" ... I praise you, Father, Lord of heaven and earth, because you have hidden these things from the wise and learned, and revealed them to little children. Yes, Father, for this was your good pleasure" (Matthew 11:25).

The wedding was over and the Christmas season was upon us. As if we didn't have enough to deal with, our sweet Ellie, now thirteen years old, was constantly talking about the orphan crisis and adoption. One of her nicknames is "Ellie Does Stuff Mestas," because she always does whatever it takes to accomplish her goal. She never gives up! She continued to read everything she could find about adoption and orphans, and she kept telling us that she felt God still had more children planned for our family. In fact, she was pretty sure there was a baby girl in China waiting for us. In one of the adoption information packets we received, there was a video with Steven Curtis and Mary Beth Chapman talking about their adoption journey to China. Ellie watched it more than 100 times. She was so persistent and passionate, and when she would tell us about the baby girls being left to die in China, tears would stream down her cheeks. We explained that we just couldn't pursue another adoption because we were out of work and had no money. The twins were now two years old, and I was pretty sure this was all I could handle anyway. But she wouldn't take no for an answer.

After many, many discussions and lots of prayer, Jerry and I decided to take another leap of faith to show her that we were willing to trust and see if this was indeed God's plan for us. Someone had given us $200 to purchase Christmas gifts for the kids. We had a family meeting and all agreed to send it off to America World Adoption Agency to pursue the adoption of a baby girl from China. We sent it off and prayed for the Lord's will to be done.

Several days after the wedding, I found a newspaper that Jerry had purchased for the out-of-town guests to read. It was about 1:00 a.m. and I tossed it in the trash. But I heard that familiar whisper, *"Look in the want ads."* I thought that was weird, but then I heard it again. So I took the paper out of the trash and my eyes fell on an ad for a sales position for a company providing security and specialty equipment to police and various law enforcement agencies. This immediately caught my attention, because Jerry had over twenty-five years of experience in law enforcement, and had spent the last two years in sales with his friend's company. I circled the ad with a bright highlighter and left it on his desk chair for him to find in the morning. He sent his resume for the job and was hired! It was now January 2007, two years, three months, and eleven days since he had lost his job. But who was counting?

He was hired as a salesman for the California, Nevada, and Arizona territory, which required extensive travel. It was a large pay cut from his previous job, but we were hopeful that he would be successful because of his experience and contacts from working as a police officer in California for twenty years. It would also give him the opportunity to visit with his family on a regular basis. We were happy to have a permanent job and were in awe that a newspaper that I pulled out of the trash because of a whisper revealed his new job!

Shortly after Jerry started the new job, we got an e-mail from America World Adoption Agency. It said, "We regret to inform you that you are no longer qualified to adopt from China. According to China's requirements and status of your timeline in the referral period you will have aged out of the program." I remembered many times in my life being told I was too young to do something, but this was my first experience being told I was too old. I was forty-eight years old and Jerry was fifty-five years old.

I called a family meeting and shared this news with everyone. It appeared God had closed this door and we were not going to adopt a little girl from China. I reminded them we had answered God's call to care for the orphans by adopting the twins, and with five children we should be content. We were too old, we had no money and now that Jerry had a job, we needed to work on paying down the debt that we had accumulated.

Well, Ellie just lost it! She began to cry and insisted that God was not finished with our adoptions. She stormed up to her room and we didn't see her until the next day. When she came down in the morning, her eyes and face were swollen from crying so much. My heart broke. I hugged her and told her I was so sorry that she was so disappointed, but that she had to understand we just couldn't adopt any more children. Again I told her, "We are too old, we have no money and we have a full quiver. Besides that, we have debt from being out of work these past two years and we have to pay it all off now that Papa got a job. We can't afford $30,000 to adopt from China!" She looked at me with her puffy eyes and swollen face and said, "I just know God has told me that we are going to adopt more children. I feel it in my heart. Maybe it's not China, but I know this is what He has put on my heart. They must be someplace else."

I tried to console her by telling her we thought the Lord might be leading us to start an adoption and orphan care ministry at our church. We heard that *FamilyLife Today®, Focus on the Family* and Show Hope were partnering together to become advocates for the orphan and we were going to join them in this new ministry, The Christian Alliance for Orphans. We wanted to encourage other families to adopt and get involved in orphan care. I thought this was the next logical step in ministry for us and she would be happy to hear it. But she wasn't consoled at all. She looked at me with that stubborn "You are not listening to me" Ellie face.

I know that God often speaks to me through my children. I have been convicted of my own sin and shortcomings many times, and have had to ask their forgiveness on more occasions than I care to remember. I honestly believe God has given me children to teach me more about life than I could ever teach them. I want to intentionally listen to what they have to say. They are wise and sincere and they take me places I would never go without them. I needed to go to the Lord in prayer.

Trust in the LORD with all your heart and lean not on your own understanding; in all your ways acknowledge him, and he will make your paths straight (Proverbs 3:5-6).

8 Lord, Show Me Your Will

Call to Me and I will answer you, and I will tell you great and mighty things, which you do not know (Jeremiah 33:3 NASB).

Have you ever felt you needed to call a friend but didn't know why? I woke up Friday morning, February 2, 2007 with a very strong feeling that I needed to call on my Heavenly Father. It was like a whisper calling me, saying, *"Come, I have something to tell you!"* It was very unusual for me to wake up before anyone else. The kids usually come to wake me up. I fixed a cup of tea, and went to the kitchen table with my Bible to call on Him.

I was feeling convicted about how I had responded to Ellie. Because she was so upset, in the back of my mind, I wondered if God really was telling her that we were supposed to adopt again. I needed to talk to Him about it.

This was my prayer: "Good morning, Lord, I am coming before You with a burdened heart. I am begging You to speak to me right now. You saw my Ellie so upset. I don't want her to keep hoping and waiting for us to adopt again if this is not Your will. I don't want to teach my children to make decisions based on humanistic logic or my opinion. I don't want to assume I know Your plans without consulting You. Lord, You saw the e-mail; we are too old to adopt. You know our bank account, we have no money and we have debt. I feel so ashamed that we have not been better stewards of all You have provided. And Lord, You know our hearts. We are not against receiving Your blessings, but it just looks like we are done. Lord, will You please show me in Your Word that we are finished with adoption, so that I can tell Ellie with confidence that it is Your will and not mine? Please Father, when I open Your Word, I beg You to answer me."

I opened my Bible, fully expecting the Lord to speak to me. It opened to Job 42. My first thought was, *"Oh, no, not Job!"* As I began to read, it was as if the words were illuminated on the page. And this is what it said:

Then Job replied to the LORD: "I know that you can do all things; no plan of yours can be thwarted. You asked, 'Who is this that obscures my counsel without knowledge?' Surely I spoke of things I did not understand, things too wonderful for me to know."

I gasped and could not believe my eyes. I had just told the Lord I thought we were finished adopting and that I wanted to be sure it was His plan. This made perfect sense as a response. Who am I to counsel Ellie without His knowledge? He can do all things, and nothing will stand in His way of the plans He has for us. Not age or logic or lack of money. I read on, with my eyes wide open, and my heart began racing.

"You said, 'Listen now, and I will speak; I will question you, and you shall answer me.' My ears had heard of you but now my eyes have seen you. Therefore I despise myself and repent in dust and ashes."

I just cried out to Him with questions and begged Him to give me answers. We had just been on a miraculous journey of watching Him perform so many miracles. I can honestly say my ears had heard of Him, but now my eyes have seen Him. I felt ashamed that I presumed to know His plan and felt convicted. I felt like He was telling me I should repent in dust and ashes. Tears began to stream down my face as I read on.

After the LORD had said these things to Job, he said to Eliphaz the Temanite, "I am angry with you and your two friends, because you have not spoken of me what is right, as my servant Job has ... You have not spoken of me what is right ..."

Again I felt as though the Lord was speaking directly to me. I was not speaking of Him what is right. I must have faith and trust Him. I am always to seek and speak truth of His righteousness. When I don't understand or things don't make sense, trust in HIM. He has a plan and I don't know what it is.

After Job had prayed for his friends, the LORD made him

prosperous again and gave him twice as much as he had before. ...
THE LORD BLESSED THE LATTER PART OF JOB'S LIFE MORE
THAN THE FIRST (emphasis added).

Lord, are You telling me Job was blessed twice as much in the latter part of his life because I just told You we are too old? Could it be You are telling me You are going to bless us with more children in the latter part of our lives too? The next verse that lit up on the page was this:

And he also had seven sons and three daughters. The first daughter he named Jemimah, the second KEZIAH and the third KEREN-Happuch. Nowhere in all the land were there found women as beautiful as Job's daughters, and their father granted them an inheritance along with their brothers. After this Job lived a hundred and forty years; he saw his children and their children to the fourth generation. And so he died, old and full of years (emphasis added).

By now, tears were streaming down my face and I knew I was in the presence of the Lord. Again I asked Him, "Lord, what are You telling me? Why are these two names appearing to be lit up on the page? What do You mean they were granted an inheritance? Girls in those days did not get an inheritance. What are You telling me, Lord?"

And I heard Him speak!

"YOU GO RESCUE MY DAUGHTERS, KEZIAH AND KEREN. YOU TEACH THEM TO KNOW ME, SO THAT THEY WILL RECEIVE THE INHERITANCE OF MY KINGDOM. I HAVE PLANS FOR YOUR OLD AGE!"

There I sat at my kitchen table, trembling and in awe that I was in the presence of the Lord. He was speaking answers, directly responding to my prayer. It was so surreal. I sat there for a long time, looking at my Bible and crying.

I finally got up and started my day, but I was in a fog. I got breakfast ready for everyone and was very quiet. I couldn't even talk for awhile. As I was quietly going through my day, I was still praying and asking God if I had really heard Him right. Then I felt like He impressed on me that Keziah and Keren were twin girls. I was trying to process what had happened and figure out how to explain it to everyone. I knew I had to call a family meeting.

I called Melissa and asked her to come over right away for a meeting, because I had to tell everyone something very important. She said she couldn't make it right away, but would come as soon as possible. She got scared and asked if I had bad news. I assured her it wasn't bad, but she had to come as soon as possible. I decided to have a meeting with everyone else and tell her later. Everyone came to the table, looking at me with wide eyes and concerned anticipation.

I took my Bible out and went through exactly what had happened and what I heard. "God spoke to me this morning, and I have to tell you all what He said. God told me we are supposed to adopt again. He already gave me the names, Keziah and Keren, and I think they are twin girls." Everyone was staring at me and they began to cry too. Ellie was ecstatic and Jerry said, "Well, if we are supposed to adopt again, we better get started right away. We're not getting any younger!"

We had planned to have a game night, but now we decided to get on the computer and start some research. We had absolutely no idea where to begin. Ellie had all kinds of information she had been collecting. She pulled up the *FamilyLife Today®* website, and we listened to a radio broadcast of a testimony of one of their employees who had just gotten home in January with two children adopted from Ethiopia. They worked with the Gladney Center for Adoption out of Texas and praised them. Then they explained that because Ethiopia had just opened, the process was moving very quickly. This piqued our interest, so we decided to go to their website.

Ellie got right on their Ethiopia adoption page. I didn't even know where Ethiopia was, so she started to research it. I went to the kitchen to get some drinks and she suddenly yelled, "Mama, come quick!" There is a city in Ethiopia named "KEREN." (It is actually in Eritrea, but was once part of Ethiopia.) Then a few minutes later, she saw the blog of another family that just adopted a little girl from Ethiopia. Her name was KEZIAH! We were absolutely amazed. We had never heard of those names before.

The Lord had revealed both of those names to us only seven hours earlier, and now they were both linked to Ethiopia as we were researching adoption. Our sweet Ellie said, "Mama and Papa, I don't think this is a coincidence. Both of those names were just linked to Ethiopia and I think God wants us to adopt Keziah and Keren from there." We were in awe and agreed to pursue it further.

We went back to the Gladney Ethiopia adoption page and started to look at the costs. For one child it was approximately $18,000, for a second $5,000, and only $1,800 for a third. We knew God had already told us we were adopting twin girls, but when I saw it was only $1,800 for a third child to be rescued, I instantly felt in my heart that we were supposed to get three children. I told Jerry and Ellie and they laughed. I said, "We don't have money for one, so what's three? If the Lord is really calling us to do this, He is going to provide." So we all agreed to step out in faith and proceed to adopt twin girls and a sibling under the age of four years old. The boys had just turned four and we didn't want to adopt out of birth order.

We decided to fill out the Gladney application and began the process. We were ready to hit "send," when we came upon our first hurdle. They required a payment of $250 with the application. I immediately responded, "That's it; we have to wait. We don't have $250." Jerry leaned over to his desk and pulled out a credit card. He said, "There is $500 available credit on this. I think we should go ahead and send in this application. We are putting out the fleece and if God is really calling us to adopt, He will send us the money to pay for it. We are not going to put another penny into it unless He makes it clear." We all agreed, we laid hands on the keyboard, praying for God to show us His plan, and hit the "send" button. Needless to say, it was quite an eventful day and I was exhausted!

Melissa came over the next morning and we sat at the kitchen table with my Bible open, as I explained what the Lord had revealed to me. She teared up and said, "Okay, Mom, this is really weird, but I guess we'll see what happens."

Then I called my dearest friend and homeschool mentor, Beth Herbert, to come over right away. She is that special friend and confidante that is a blessing and rare to find. The kind you can call on anytime. She always speaks truth and points me to the Word of God when I need it. I call her my witness as she has had a front row seat in my life for twelve years. Her daughter Amanda and Ellie have been the best of friends since they were two years old.

They too sat in awe, as we sat at the kitchen table for the third time, sharing this revelation. We all agreed the Lord had been faithful in showing us many miracles in the past and we were excited to see what was going to happen next. This was going to be huge if it came true!

9 Miraculous Provision

"I know that you can do all things; no plan of yours can be thwarted. My ears had heard of you but now my eyes have seen you" (Job 42:2, 5).

It was Monday, February 19, 2007 and we got a call from Debra Parris with the Gladney Center for Adoption. She had received our application and needed to conduct a telephone interview. She said she noticed that we specified three children under the age of four and twin girls. She asked why we were so specific. I didn't know how she was going to react when I told her God had clearly spoken to me, but I proceeded to share my testimony with her. She was amazed and luckily didn't hang up.

She explained that for three children the total cost would be approximately $30,000, and because the Ethiopian program was moving so quickly, we could be home with our children within six months. Then she said, "Now this is the worst part of my job. I have to ask, do you have the money to get started right now?" To which I responded without any hesitation, "No, we didn't even have the $250 application fee." She suggested we get a loan or second mortgage and informed us the government offered a tax credit for adoptions. Since we were adopting three children, we would qualify for approximately $30,000 in tax credits that would enable us to pay the loans off over the next five years. I told her we were already maxed out on our loans, credit cards, and had a second mortgage, because we had been out of work the past two years.

She asked how we were planning to get the money. The program moves very quickly and most of the paperwork expires within one year. We had to make sure we had all the money before we could proceed. I told her we had been on an amazing journey of God performing miracles in our lives. We already agreed that we were going to pray and wait for Him to give us another one. If He truly was calling us to adopt these children, then He was going to provide the money somehow. We had absolutely no idea how, but we were going to wait and trust Him.

She started asking questions about our adoption of the twin boys that she noticed on our application. She asked what we did with the tax credit from adopting them in 2003. I explained they were a "Special Needs" adoption and we did not pay any adoption fees for them. Jerry always says we adopted two children for the price of none. Our accountant, who had two degrees on his office wall; the other being an attorney, so he obviously knows his stuff, told us we did not qualify for the tax credit when we adopted them. He explained that, because we did not pay any adoption fees, we could not apply for the credit. She was quiet for a minute and said, "I don't think that's right. You should have gotten the Special Needs tax credit. You need to check on that." I immediately called our accountant at home. It was 10:00 p.m. and when I explained everything to him, he said he would check on it first thing in the morning.

Within twenty-four hours of telling Debra we were going to wait for a miracle, the telephone rang. It was Tuesday, February 20, 2007, 11:00 a.m. and it was our accountant. He said, "Eileen, it 'appears' there has been a terrible mistake. The entire office worked on your file this morning. I told them somebody's pelt is going to hang on the mantel. I have an amendment in my hand that I am faxing to you right now for your signatures. It is for your 2003, 2004 and 2005 tax returns for a "Special Needs" adoption tax credit. YOU NOW HAVE $20,000 COMING TO YOU WITHIN THE NEXT 8 to 10 WEEKS!"

I started to cry and screamed into the phone, "This is the miracle! This is a miracle from God!" To which he replied, "Eileen, it's more of a miracle than you realize. You only had until April 15, 2007 to file an amendment to the 2003 tax return due to a statute of limitations. If you hadn't found this money before then, the government would never have to give it to you! We were less than two months from the deadline."

It was as if the Holy Spirit spoke through me and I said,"God hid that money all this time and revealed it for such a time as this. We are going to adopt three children from Ethiopia!"

I immediately hung up and called Debra at Gladney. I screamed into the phone, "Debra, God gave us the miracle!! We have $20,000 coming to us from the Special Needs tax credit. It's the miracle we were praying for. And He delivered in less than twenty-four hours." She started screaming in the phone right back at me. We were both doing the happy dance. Then she said, "OK, so now I am faxing your next set of application forms today and you need to return them within two weeks with a check for $5,000. We need to get going before the Ethiopian government closes for the rainy season." I told her we weren't getting the money for 8 to 10 weeks and we didn't have it. She said, "Well, let's see what God is going to do next then. Hurry and let's get this thing going."

A few days later, I was hit with a spiritual attack. Fear started to rear its ugly head again. It is always interesting how quickly Satan tries to jump right in and thwart God's plans. We were taking the Dave Ramsey finance class at the time and I was stressing about our debt. I started thinking, *How are we going to afford three more children with all this debt and a salary cut?* We were all at the dinner table and I said, "Hey, guys, this is really crazy stuff happening. Maybe we should wait to proceed with adoption. We have all this debt and that money is really ours, right? Maybe we should use it to pay down on our debt and wait until we get it paid off, then save some money? God doesn't like us to be in debt, right? And isn't that what Dave Ramsey would say?" Ellie and Jerry looked at me like I was crazy and said NO!

Then I was rattled back to reality by Jonathan's response. "Hey, Mom, I think God made it pretty clear that He hid that money and revealed it for this adoption. If you don't obey Him, He's going to get really mad at you." I was so surprised to hear him say that and he was so sure of himself. I looked at everyone and said, "Okay, then, is everyone in agreement to proceed with this adoption? Everything has been happening so fast; it's only been two weeks since it all started, and it just seems crazy. Sometimes I wonder if I am crazy or if God really is talking to me." Everyone agreed we must proceed with this adoption.

Then I said, "Here is the deal. Let's not say anything to anyone yet. If word gets out about God talking to me this time, everyone is going to think I am really crazy. They are going to come with the white jackets for me. Let's just wait and see what happens, like we did when we adopted the boys. No one knew we were in the adoption process until we got the call to go to the hospital." We all looked at each other for a few minutes and they agreed to appease me. "Mum's the word until further notice!" Here we go again, embarking on another faith journey.

The following Sunday, February 26, 2007, we were sitting in the back row at church. I was still trying to process all that had taken place that week. The sermon was from Mark 4, where Jesus was teaching many things by parables. I specifically heard verses 9-12, *Then Jesus said, "He who has ears to hear, let him hear." When he was alone, the Twelve and the others around him asked him about the parables. He told them, "The secret of the kingdom of God has been given to you. But to those on the outside everything is said in parables so that, "'they may be ever seeing but never perceiving, and ever hearing but never understanding; otherwise they might turn and be forgiven!'"* And it was then that I heard the whisper, *"Eileen, I want you to* **TELL THIS STORY** *of what I have done in your life this week. I want you to share everything I am going to do on this adoption journey. I want my people to SEE the miracles and HEAR what I want them to do. I want everyone to know this is ME at work and not you and Jerry.* **Tell this story** *to bring glory and honor to Me!"*

Again, I started to tremble as I leaned over to Jerry and said, "God just told me to share this story of what He did this week." He looked over at me and said, "But you just told us all not to say anything." I answered, "I know, but God just spoke to me and told me we have to tell. And I think He wants us to start right now. We have to tell the whole church what happened." To which he responded, "You can't do that! You can't just get up and share without approval." I looked at him with what he calls "that look" and said, "Jerry, God said we have to!" So, he rolled his eyes and went to talk with a fellow elder, Don Albright. When he explained to Don that we felt led by the Lord to share something, he agreed to let us speak at the end of the service. This had never been done before in our church.

I stood before the congregation, and with tears and trembling, opened my Bible. I shared what the Lord had shown me in Job 42, and that we were to step out in faith and adopt three children from Ethiopia. Then I shared the miracle of Him revealing $20,000 within twenty-four hours of our speaking to the adoption agency. You could hear a loud gasp and many began to cry. I explained that the money would take 8 to 10 weeks to arrive, and we needed $5,000 within two weeks to start the process, before the rainy season and government closures in Ethiopia. I asked that they all join us in prayer and to be ready to SEE GOD as we began this new faith journey. Everyone was used to watching God work in our family by now. They had been praying for us through all of our previous faith journeys.

The service had ended, and we were gathering the kids, when a man came up to us. He had tears in his eyes and said, "We are just visiting here today and want to thank you for sharing this amazing testimony. I know this is crazy, but God told me to give this to you to help get your little girls home." He handed Jerry a check for $500. A few minutes later, another friend, Scott, came to Jerry and said, "I know this is weird, but I think God just told me to give this to you. It's not much, but I hope it helps get your girls home." He handed Jerry a check for $500. God delivered $1,000 to us that day. We never expected that to happen.

As a result of telling this story on Sunday, the elders sent a church wide e-mail that the following Sunday there would be an opportunity for a love offering for our family's adoption. This had also never been done in our church before. That following Sunday they collected $1,800, and the church gave us the difference to cover the $5,000 required to begin our process. So at the end of that service they gave us a check totaling $4,000. Three weeks ago we had absolutely no money and now we had $25,000. How do you explain that without using the word MIRACLE in the sentence!?

We completed the paperwork, attached the check and sent it to the Gladney Center for Adoption. We made appointments for all the physicals, CIS, passports, FBI fingerprints, and the journey began. We also sent out request for prayer support letters to friends and family, sharing this amazing story with them. We were on a new journey of faith, and many people told us they were experiencing a revival in their own faith as a result of SEEING GOD at work.

We had a few bumps in the road over the next few weeks. It turned out I have no fingerprints. I have the reputation of being a clean freak and I had actually cleaned my prints right off. After two trips to CIS and FBI clearance, they finally approved my application, since I had no other criminal records. I was put in the category of an amputee or a burn victim.

We still needed $15,000, which included approximately $10,000 for travel expenses. There would be three of us flying to Ethiopia, and six of us flying home, plus two weeks of hotel and expenses. We decided to send a grant request to Show Hope. Steven Curtis Chapman is one my absolute favorite Christian artists. He and his wife, Mary Beth, have three biological children and adopted three more from China. They founded the Show Hope organization that provides grants to Christian families to help with adoption expenses. We had been following their ministry for several years and never dreamed we would be applying for a grant from them. We were shocked and so grateful when they approved our application and gave us a substantial grant.

Another day there was a $3,000 payment due to Gladney. By now, sharing our progress testimony had become a regular part of our worship service at church, as we were asked to share updates every Sunday. I intended to ask for prayer for this need, but when we were called before the church, I clearly heard God say, *"Don't say a word about the money you need. Trust Me!"* I didn't say a word. As the service was ending and we were getting ready to leave, my friend Dena came over to me and was crying.

She said, "We have wanted to help you guys earlier, but I just never had peace about it. This has never happened to me before. When you were sharing earlier, God spoke to me. He told me to give this to you and He even said the exact amount to give to you." She handed me a check and walked away, still crying. I tucked it in my purse and opened it when we got home. It was $3,000! I called her at home and told her how I had intended to share the need but God told me not to. She was in awe that God had spoken so clearly to her and told her to give this gift. We both just cried as we felt the power of God's Spirit move among us.

For the rest of our journey the Lord was having many people

in the church contribute to our adoption fund-raising. Little Anna Brown was five years old, and she began collecting coins from their couch cushions and her big brothers' pockets. She handed us an envelope with $6.42 and a picture she drew of our waiting children. There was such an outpouring of love and support from every family in our small church of twenty-four families. Several of them were giving us checks once a month and getting support from their family and friends as well. The Lord was so quickly pouring His provision on us to pay for all the expenses to adopt these precious children, and working in the lives of so many people. The Scriptures tell us pure religion is to care for orphans and widows in their distress. Not everyone is called to adopt, but everyone is called to care for them. God was providing opportunities for our entire church, family, and friends to obey His command. Everyone was a part of rescuing these orphans. I am surprised we don't all have fractured jaw bones from all the jaw-dropping miracles we witnessed.

The Lord used Job 42 to tell us to begin this adoption journey. I see another lesson He taught from this chapter, in verses 10-12. The Lord restored Job's family and wealth in the latter part of his life. *After Job had prayed for his friends, the LORD made him prosperous again and gave him twice as much as he had before. All his brothers and sisters and everyone who had known him before came and ate with him in his house. They comforted him and consoled him over all the trouble the LORD had brought upon him, and each one gave him a piece of silver and a gold ring. The LORD blessed the latter part of Job's life more than the first* (emphasis added).

The Lord could have restored his wealth in many ways, but He chose to use the people in Job's life to do it. All his brothers, sisters, and everyone who knew him brought him silver and gold. That is exactly what the Lord did to provide all the money we needed for this adoption. We did not have one penny when we started this journey. In fact, we had debt from being out of work for several years. But that did not thwart His plan. He is our provider and He chooses to use His people to accomplish His will.

10 Referral From Ethiopia

I wait for the LORD, my soul waits, and in HIS word I put my hope (Psalm 130:5, emphasis added).

Do not be anxious about anything, but in everything, by prayer and petition, with thanksgiving, present your requests to God. And the peace of God, which transcends all understanding, will guard your hearts and your minds in Christ Jesus (Philippians 4:6-7).

One morning in July, I got a call from our caseworker, Mary Thottukadavil. She explained that all of our paperwork was approved and ready to fax to the Ethiopian office for our referral. But there was a problem that we had to address. All of our paperwork requested twin girls and a sibling under the age of four years old. Mary's boss, Scott Brown, the Director of the Ethiopian program, had been in contact with their Ethiopian staff. Mr. Belay told him they were working with five government-run orphanages, and there were no twins with a sibling available. Mary also told me that we didn't qualify for this children's age group because of our ages, and we needed to be open to whatever referral they would give us. Because the international adoption paperwork is only good for one year, we were taking the risk that all of our paperwork would expire, and we would lose the money we had already invested. At this point we were about five months into the process, and the government was going to close for the rainy season for two months.

We spent forty-five minutes on the phone, as I tried to convince her I had absolutely no peace about changing anything on our paperwork. We had been watching God perform miracles on this entire journey and it all started when He told me to adopt twin girls. My tongue could not say a word about changing anything.

I finally said, "Mary, you do whatever you have to on your paperwork. But we are going to watch God perform another miracle. I just know it." She said, "Okay, I can change this paperwork to state you will take another referral?" I repeated, "You do what you have to do on your papers, but we are going to watch God perform a miracle!" With that, we finally said goodbye. I was discouraged and a seed of doubt began to stir in me. Then I prayed to the Lord again, asking that His will be done and that I would accept whatever that was.

Two weeks later, Friday, August 10, 2007, Ellie came down for breakfast very upset. She proceeded to tell us that she'd had a nightmare. She dreamt that she was spending the night with her best friend, Amanda, and our referral call came in. In her dream, we got twin girls, two years old, and their baby brother, five months old. We were so excited that we got on the plane and went to Ethiopia without her. She was as upset as if we had really left without her. Then she said she was not going anywhere with Amanda until after our adoption was final. I assured her it was just a dream and we would never go to Ethiopia without her. We needed her to carry one of the babies. Besides, I reminded her of the forty-five minute phone call from Mary T. just two weeks earlier, telling us we were not going to get twins and a sibling anyway.

Within minutes the phone rang, and it was Amanda. Ellie didn't even want to talk to her because she was still upset. But I made her get on the phone and told her she was just being silly. We were in the middle of a 100-degree heat wave and Amanda invited her to go ice skating that afternoon. Ellie asked me, "Are you sure we don't have anything going on today? Are you sure I shouldn't stay home?" I told her she was being ridiculous and encouraged her to go have fun with Amanda. She reluctantly agreed and they picked her up a few minutes later. She walked out the door in an unusually weird mood.

It wasn't more than twenty minutes later that the telephone rang. It was Mary T. from Gladney. She sounded very happy and I assumed she had another issue to talk to me about. Then, all of a sudden it hit me, and I screamed, "Mary? Is this 'THE' call?

AHHHHHHHH!" And then again, "Is this *the* call?"

"Jerry! Come here! Hurry!" He thought someone had died or was at least seriously injured. I was really screaming. Jeremiah and James came running into the kitchen and hid under the table. Jonathan ran into the kitchen with a frightened look on his face. My mind was racing. I had to calm down. I had to calm them down. Then she said, "Eileen, have your family get to your computer, because we have your referral." Then in my mind I thought, *Oh, no, we didn't get the twins*. Then I started yelling again, "Wait, we can't open the computer yet! We have to get everyone here! Jerry, Mary has our referral! Call Melissa, Grandma, Grandpa, and Ellie … Oh, no, Ellie is with Amanda! Oh, Ellie's dream!! Ellie was with Amanda in her dream when you called with our referral!" I was rambling ninety miles an hour and poor Mary was listening to me screaming all of this in her ear. Jerry and Jonathan got on their cell phones and started calling everyone.

Jerry called Beth, Amanda's mom, and told her Ellie had to get home immediately because the referral was coming. Beth and I had discussed Ellie's dream. Ellie and Amanda had just put on their skates and were about to step out on the ice, when Beth ran into the rink and literally started screaming, "Ellie, Ellie, you have to get home. The referral call is in!!!"

Ellie looked at her with wide eyes welling up with tears, and started screaming at Amanda. "YOU! I'm not supposed to be here with you!" Amanda stood in shock for a moment, as Ellie hobbled out of the rink on her skates as fast as she could. She tore her skates off and ran out to the parking lot where Melissa and Randy were already waiting. Ellie came in the door in tears and shaking. In the meantime, I was telling Mary all about her dream while we were waiting for everyone to arrive.

We had already planned that when we got our referral, we would not open it until everyone was there. It is like being a witness to a live birth. You just can't play "rewind;" you have to be there. And what a miracle it was that all ten of us were there on a Friday afternoon. Only an awesome God who has each of our hairs numbered could have orchestrated such a scene.

Suddenly, we were all there in the kitchen. Melissa, armed with her camera, taking pictures, and Jonathan taking video. We all gathered around the computer, opened the e-mail and could not believe our eyes. We scrolled down to see beautiful five-month-old twin girls and their two-year-old brother! We all burst into tears and we instantly fell in love! "This is exciting, God is happy," said Jeremiah. "This is amazing," said James. We were all in shock and bawling. My dad said, "I just can't believe this!" How incredible that Ellie's dream came true, only with the ages reversed.

As we were staring at their photos, Mary started to tell us all about them. Our new son was two years and eleven months old. His given name was Abel. We decided to name him Josiah Abel. I was studying Kings in my Bible study during this time and King Josiah is noted to be one of the greatest kings, because all the days of his life he followed after God. He never strayed to the left or the right. This is our prayer for Josiah Abel.

The first twinette (because we have twin boys, the girls are referred to as the twinettes) is Selam, which means "Peace" in Amharic, their native language. She is now Keziah Selam. We found out after research that Keziah means "Beautiful Restoration." The second twinette is Fikir, which means "Love" in Amharic. She is now Keren Fikir. After research we learned Keren was the name of the most beautiful color in Job's day. It is a cinnamon color, like the color of their skin.

How amazing is our God that He is so detailed. On February 2, 2007 He told me to go rescue His daughters Keziah and Keren. They were not even born until February 15, 2007, and we got the call from Gladney which started the process on February 19. The names He gave them described their beautiful restoration and the color of their skin.

After we calmed down and were absorbing all of this, I just had to say it. "Mary, just two weeks ago you told me we were not going to get twins with a sibling. Do you remember?" To which she responded, "Oh, Eileen, I will never forget it. We were on the phone for almost an hour, and I told you Scott told me to call you. We had sent your paperwork to our Ethiopian office and it got kicked back to us. Belay, our representative in Ethiopia told us to have you change your referral request, because he knew this was not going to happen. After I hung up with you I changed the paperwork and I faxed it back to Belay. Eileen, everyone here at Gladney has been dying to call you for two weeks, but we had to wait for all the paperwork to be approved first. I feel so privileged to be part of this adoption. We are so amazed. Eileen, within forty-five minutes of your paperwork arriving at our Ethiopian office, your three children arrived at the door! Belay was in shock and tears. He said, 'As soon as I saw them come through the door I knew these were the Mestas children. This was the first time I did not have to match a referral for a family. God did it before they even got here!'" Do you see God? Only He could orchestrate this miracle!

The rainy season had begun and the government was closing, so we had to wait until November to go get our beautiful babies. During this time we did some work on the house in preparation for three more children. My life was about to take another major transformation, but I really had no idea to what extreme. I was afraid this was more than I could handle. I was forty-eight years old, and preparing for life with five children ages four years and under, including two infants in diapers! We were on another faith journey!

Testimony of Mary Thottukadavil, our caseworker from Gladney:

I remember when I first spoke to Eileen regarding what ages and gender they were open to adopting from Ethiopia. This is a story I continue to share as one of my favorite "God stories" when working at Gladney. Even though I truly believe that every adoption is a God story, this one is filled with such miracles that I constantly found myself picking my jaw up from the floor as I watched the impossible become possible.

As the Mestas family's caseworker, my job was to make sure they understood the rules of how long the adoption process could possibly take in receiving a child referral in the age range they were requesting. I must admit, when I saw that they were so specific in their child request, asking for up to three children under four years of age, and that two of them would be female twins, I knew I had to give them the "talk!" The talk involves me explaining how being that specific on the dossier paperwork may not be wise, as they could likely be waiting for a very long time and their documents could expire (as per rules in Ethiopia). I was trying to be as realistic as I could be with Eileen when it came to giving estimates of how long they could possibly be waiting for three children.

At that time, I knew we didn't have any twins under Gladney's foster care, and worried that we may not receive twins anytime soon. I knew that the Mestases hoped to receive their referral within the same timeline as the rest, who were open to a single child of either gender. So naturally, speaking with Eileen, I needed to warn her of this reality—that they could possibly be waiting a very LONG time. There have been times that I have been misquoted, and had to console adoptive parents who expected to have their child referral within a certain period of time, upset that I didn't keep to what they *thought* I had said. I remember Eileen saying to me, "Mary, I know you are going to think I am crazy, but God has told our family that we are going to be adopting twins and they are going to be girls!" I remember that Eileen was talking a mile a minute! For those of you that know her, you know what I mean, but she really is a joy to listen to! I appreciate her tenacity, boldness and great sense of humor so much.

She told me how she had adopted twin boys and knew that God had His hand in that adoption. She went on to say that they were taking another step of faith and believed what God had told them, even though it sounded crazy and they didn't have all financial funding for it yet!

I do remember listening to Eileen and admiring how BOLD she was in her faith in Jesus, and how she didn't feel okay accepting a referral for children outside of what God had told their family. I am a believer as well, so I didn't think she was crazy at all, but I do admit I had no idea that everything would happen the way it did! God is so good!

Shortly after that call, I happened to speak with Belay, in our Ethiopian office, over the phone, and I remember discussing other cases as we normally did; and right before I hung up the phone, I told him about the phone call I had just had with Eileen. I told him that the Mestas family said that God had told their family that they would be adopting from Ethiopia, and in addition to that, they would be receiving a referral for twin girls and possibly a third child. After saying it I remember pausing, expecting to hear Belay laugh and remind me that it would be better for them to keep their preferences open, but he did not do that! He said, "What did you say?" I repeated myself and he said in a shocked voice, "Um, well, actually Mary, I just met a mother today who shared that she was interested in placing her twin baby girls for adoption." He went on to explain that he directed her to a local government orphanage. This is what birth parents are supposed to do if placing their child for adoption.

I remember saying, "Are you serious, Belay?!" and he said with a chuckle in his voice, "Yes!" I thought, *Wow, everything that God told the Mestas family is coming true! How amazing is God in His timing of things!* I asked Belay, "Do you know if she has any other children?" I was thinking in the back of my mind, what about the third child God told the Mestas family about? He said, "Well, she had a little boy with her as well, but she didn't mention anything about placing him in the orphanage when she spoke to me." In my mind, I immediately knew ... these were meant to be the Mestas children!

I could not WAIT to tell the Mestas family, but knew that the in-country staff needed to wait for the children to be placed; and do all the background research to ensure that the children would be eligible for adoption, before sharing the referral of the children with the Mestas family. I ran and told my coworkers the story and everyone was amazed! I remember anxiously awaiting the children's referral to be ready so I could make the call ... oh, what a call to make! Two weeks later, I got to make that call! From my end, the JOY that overcame the entire family was contagious. I could not stop smiling! Making that phone call was truly humbling and I can only give God the glory, as it is all truly because of Him. He knew these children were meant to be adopted by this family even before they were born. He knew the Mestas family would be able to be a voice for who He is and how He loves His children and provides for them. I was so blessed to be a part of this family's adoption journey and witness the miracle of how God creates forever families. The Mestas family is an incredibly loving family who I will always admire for being unwavering in their faith, bold to share the good news of Jesus Christ, honest about their hard times, while praising God even in the storm and thanking Him for His providence. I look forward to seeing what God has planned for the lives of Josiah Abel, Keziah Selam, and Keren Fikir!

11 Ethiopia, Here We Come

Now to him who is able to do immeasurably more than all we ask or imagine, according to his power that is at work within us, to him be glory in the church and in Christ Jesus throughout all generations, for ever and ever! Amen (Ephesians 3:20-21).

On November 1, 2007, the courts approved our adoption. *Behold, children are a heritage from the LORD, The fruit of the womb is a reward (Psalm 127:3).* As I reflected back over the adoption journey, I couldn't help but feel overwhelmed by all the miracles that God performed and how quickly He accomplished everything. It was as if God picked me up like a dandelion in His hands and gently blew me into this adoption journey to Ethiopia. Everything was totally out of my control and more than I could handle. My heart was full of gratitude.

Jerry, Ellie and I flew out November 17, 2007 with fourteen pieces of luggage. At that time it was mandatory to stay in Ethiopia for two weeks. It was also required to bring humanitarian aid supplies for the orphanages. On top of that, we needed our own two weeks' supplies for six people, including formula for two nine-month-old babies. When we checked in at RDU they informed us we had to pay additional fees for the luggage. One suitcase alone was going to cost $540 because it was overweight. The woman suggested we split it into another bag, which would reduce the cost. We explained that it was humanitarian aid for the orphanage, and asked if they would give us a break. She said there was nothing she could do. Jonathan had just left the airport and we called to ask him to bring us another bag from home. While we waited for him we prayed.

When he arrived, we were reloading the suitcases, when the woman walked up to us and said, "I have decided not to charge you for anything. Just bring your bags over here and I'll load them up. I don't know what they will do when you get to DC, but this is all I can do." We were shocked and believe the Lord turned her heart for us. The blessings abound!

We arrived at Dulles Airport, where we switched over to Ethiopian Airlines. Of course, the agent asked for the receipt for the extra luggage. We looked at each other and just said we didn't have one. He took our passports and told us to step aside because he had to call his manager. Again, we started praying. He called Jerry over and told him it would cost an additional $380. Jerry then explained that they were full of humanitarian aid for the orphanages, and we didn't have a receipt because the agent at RDU let it go through at no charge. He literally stood there for a minute, looking at Jerry, then the man handed him our passports and said, "Okay, go ahead and have a seat." Blessings abound again. (It would have cost close to $1,000 for the extra bags.)

While waiting to board the plane, we noticed several other Americans in the crowd of Ethiopians. It's not like Ethiopia is a hot vacation spot, so we wondered if they were on an adoption journey as well. We had an hour to kill, so we started making the rounds and talking to them. It was encouraging to meet several other adoptive families. We shared adoption stories and referral photos with each other. One couple from Delaware, Bill and Michelle McConomy, were going to adopt a baby girl. Jerry told him we were getting three children, and how God had given us the miracle of providing the money we needed through the tax credit from our previous adoption. Suddenly, Bill interrupted him saying, "Hey, I just heard your story on the radio yesterday on the Crown Financial radio program. I was just telling my wife, Michelle, your story on the way to the airport today. On the broadcast you said you were going to Ethiopia in four weeks, so I figured that would be December. I never expected to meet you here today! Can you believe this?"

As it turned out, we were all staying at the Hilton Hotel in Addis Ababa and spent a lot of time together. Our first Sunday there, we were not able to leave the hotel, because all the roads were closed for the Great Ethiopian Run with 30,000 runners. So, the McConomys invited us to have a poolside church service with them. We were in awe of what the Lord was doing in our lives and felt humbled by it. We sat together with our new babies, our Bibles, a bottle of water, and a piece of bread for Communion. It was a beautiful two-hour service of feasting on the Scriptures and shedding tears together. We bonded as dear friends and still keep in touch. In fact, I asked them to contribute to this story and Bill wrote his version of our meeting and airport experience.

At the Airport by Bill McConomy

My wife, Michelle, and I were on our way to adopt our daughter from Ethiopia. We arrived early at the airport. We checked in and found a nice quiet set of seats by the gate to relax and wait for boarding. We couldn't help but notice that the other people waiting at the gate with us were of African descent and dressed in formal Ethiopian clothing. We wondered if they were returning home or going to visit friends or relatives. Because of our physical appearance, we knew we stuck out like sore thumbs. We wondered if our purpose for going to Ethiopia crossed their minds as they waited alongside us.

Soon, several traditional American singles, couples, and families joined the gateway gathering. We knew Ethiopia wasn't your typical American vacation getaway, so we made an educated guess that others were on their way to bring home their adopted children from Ethiopia too. However, there was one couple and teen-age daughter that came to the gate that didn't remain seated quietly like the rest of us ... minding our own business.

We noticed that this husband and wife, within minutes of putting down their bags, began to introduce themselves with big smiles and happy chit-chat to everyone at the gateway seating area. If I didn't know any better, I would have thought they were running for office. They were way too friendly for us. I quickly counted how many families they had to greet before reaching us. I tried to determine how much time we had to move to different seats and politely avoid meeting people we would never talk to again.

They were in no hurry as they talked with others. At their

current pace of chit-chat, I started feeling safe in our seats on the far side of the seating area. They would never reach us before boarding time. I must have become distracted because I lost track of their progress, and the next thing I knew they were hovering over us with their big, smiling faces. Jerry and Eileen Mestas. I would never forget Eileen's name. She made sure of that. She told us her name and then pointed to her 'Eye,' and then began to lean to her side like the Tower of Pisa. 'Eye-lean.' It was quirky, but it worked. But 'what's-his-name' (Jerry) didn't have any clever tricks to help us remember his name.

I quickly realized Jerry and Eileen were a mismatched pair. They were like a brown and a yellow sock that by some kind of accident got paired up. Jerry was calm, cool, and cordial. Eileen, on the other hand, was a ball of energy and enthusiasm. I attributed most of her excitement and animation to the Ethiopian adventure ahead of us to get our adopted children. But two minutes into the conversation, I wasn't too sure it had anything to do with the adventure. Whatever it was, I wanted what she was drinking.

Eileen did most of the talking for them (hard to believe, I know). She told us about their journey to adopt, and gave a brief synopsis of every other family also waiting at the gate. Right from the beginning of their story to adopt, she explained that their journey was really God's story. It was HIS-story. Every other sentence was peppered with "God this" and "God that." I felt like she was trying to evangelize us and to eventually lead us into praying the sinner's prayer.

I told them that we were Christians too, in hopes that she wouldn't feel like she had to convert us, or convince us that God was arranging all these amazing things on their path to adoption. But my admission that we were also Christians only produced the opposite reaction that I had hoped for. Two seconds before my admission, I was pretty much a complete stranger to them. Now, I was a "brother in Christ," for whom Eileen exclaimed joyfully and with no regard for using her indoor voice. At this point, there was an awkward pause in which I thought a hug was coming my way from my long-lost "sister." Instead, this new-found connection in Christ opened up a more personal dimension of discussion.

Apparently, since we were brother and sister now, Eileen thought it was okay to begin telling me all about their financial problems on the road to adoption. As I listened politely to their predicament, I was thinking there was no way I would ever attempt to adopt under their financial circumstances. This in my mind was a confirmation of their craziness. I reasoned that they took their faith in God way too far. However, as Eileen continued to share, there was a vague sense of familiarity about their financial situation and story. I had heard this story somewhere before. As more details of the story unfolded, I suddenly realized *where* I had heard it.

Just the previous day, I was listening to the tail end of a Christian radio program that was playing pre-recorded messages from people who called in to the program to share their story of God's faithfulness in their lives. I only caught the last message of the program that aired that day. It was an amazing story of how God led a couple to adopt three children from Ethiopia, and how God hid the money from them until it was time to pay for the adoption. If they'd had the money any sooner, they would have misspent it. What impressed me so much was how this couple took steps of faith under very stressful financial conditions, without knowing where the money was coming from to pay for the adoptions. I don't have that kind of faith … especially with finances. Since we were also adopting from Ethiopia, I told the story to my wife and we discussed it on our journey to the airport.

I couldn't believe I was now sitting across from the woman who had told that amazing story that was broadcast across the entire country. At this point, I interrupted Eileen and finished her story for her. Now it was Eileen's turn to be shocked. She didn't even hear her story on the radio. She was speechless, but only for a couple of seconds. I have come to understand that very few people can make Eileen speechless. That is a feat usually reserved for God.

I remember being impressed with their openness and boldness in sharing their faith through God's story that played out in their personal lives. They wore their faith on their sleeves. They wore it well. It was clear that Jerry and Eileen loved the Lord. I remembered thinking I could use a little of their boldness in my expression of faith. In the gateway-seating-area of life I was comfortable with being quiet and blending in. It would take much more than an educated guess for someone to figure out the purpose and destination of my flight in this life.

Everyone knew what Jerry and Eileen had been drinking. And others wanted some too. It was about this time that an airport worker announced in a panicked voice for the help of a doctor or nurse. Michelle was a nurse and she jumped up to see how she could help in whatever the medical emergency was at hand. I thought Eileen was a medical professional too, because she followed right behind without any hesitation. I was about twenty yards away and had a direct line of sight, as they rushed to the aid of a mother and her unconscious child. I later found out that the child had hit her head in the bathroom and was at first fine, but later passed out. I watched as my wife tried to assess the child's condition and determine next steps as the first minute or two passed. The next thing I saw was Eileen on her knees next to the child, with one hand on the child and one hand raised above her head. Eileen began to call out the name of Jesus for help.

My view became blocked as people crowded around. Oh, brother! My first thought was that Eileen was really over the top with her faith. Her boldness was just too bold. She really needed to step aside and let people who could help practically work on the child. If she wanted to pray for the child, then she could do all the praying she needed to right from a seat in the seating area … like me.

A few minutes later, Michelle returned. I asked her what had happened to the girl and if she was able to help. She said that the child did regain consciousness. I made a sarcastic comment about Eileen's dramatic prayer in front of everyone. What was she, a faith healer too!?! Michelle then explained that she really couldn't help the girl and didn't know what else to do medically. Michelle further explained that as soon as Eileen started to pray and say the name of Jesus that the girl's eyes popped open. A soft 'Oh' escaped from my big, faithless mouth.

During the next sixteen hours of flight I contemplated the events of that morning, the big smiles of Eileen and Jerry, and their big, bold faith. My faith was faithless compared to theirs, yet we served the same God. Was I ashamed of God? I wanted to have the same boldness and excitement that they had. I wanted to share my faith with genuine excitement like them.

Jerry and Eileen are a perfect pair together. They are not mismatched socks. They are matched by God. God's feet fit very well in them. In fact, I believe God wears one brown and one yellow sock. And God is not embarrassed at all by them. This was just the beginning of a friendship and a bird's-eye view into the lives of Jerry and Eileen as they follow in God's footsteps.

12 Gotcha' Day

We arrived at the hotel after the twenty-four hour journey and took a nap. Then Ryan came to take us to meet our children. When I got out of the car to meet Belay for the first time, I started to cry. Here was this big man walking toward me with his arms wide open. He said, "So you are the famous Mestas family. I will never forget you." He too started to tear up. "I will never forget that your twins showed up right when I got the phone call from Mary. From now on whenever I see twins, I will think of you."

We went to the Gladney house to get Josiah first. We wanted to have an entire day to focus on him before we got the twinettes. He was sleeping when we arrived and Belay woke him up to introduce us. I held him first and I could not hold back my tears. I just started to weep with gratitude and overflowing joy. I didn't mean to, but my reaction scared him, and he too began to cry and reach for Belay. He was probably thinking, *Who is this crazy, crying white lady?*

Belay held him and started telling him that we were his new family. Josiah kept looking at us and Belay started to remind him of the photo album we had sent. That seemed to trigger his memory and he calmed down. I held him in my arms again, this time without crying, and we started to check his fingers and toes just like when you give birth. Yes, they were all there and he was just beautiful. He had celebrated a birthday since our referral day and was now three years old. We stayed at the Gladney house for awhile to get him warmed up to us, and then we went out to eat. He loved all the food and ate as much as Papa. For a little guy he could really eat a lot. We took him back to the hotel and gave him his first bath. He loved playing in the tub and with the toys and coloring books we had brought for him. I was so surprised and grateful that he adjusted to us so quickly. He started speaking English on the first day. His first words were "Ellie," "Dog" and "Agua." At bath time we told him water was "Agua." We speak Spanish and English, so he was already getting accustomed to the crazy Mestas life. Now that we have the Amharic language in the mix, we invented our own word for how we speak in our home. We now speak Spanglaharic: Spanish, English, and Amharic.

Josiah was doing really well until bedtime. He began to cry and tried to walk out the door. He didn't understand where he was or who he was with. He cried as I cuddled him to sleep and continued to cry throughout the night. I held him and cried with him, as I tried to imagine what he was going through. He had been through a lot of trauma in his short-lived three years. He was better in the morning and especially happy when he had pancakes and eggs for breakfast. He also took really well to Ellie and kept hugging and kissing her. His smile was illuminating.

It was time to get our baby girls and Josiah was excited to go see his baby sisters. We arrived at the Gladney baby house and Josiah had just fallen asleep. We laid him on the couch while they brought the girls to us. It worked out great that he was asleep, because we were able to focus on the girls and not make him feel left out. They were dressed in boys' clothes, but were definitely beautiful little girls. Keziah was put in my arms and she started to scream. It didn't help that I was crying too. I could not contain my joy and was in awe of what God had done. Keren was put in Jerry's arms, and she smiled for the next two weeks. She was such a happy baby. We all just held each other and cried. I instantly fell in love with my precious children. I knew without a shadow of a doubt that the Lord had given them to us as a gift and a blessing. It was only nine months earlier that I was sitting at my kitchen table and the Lord revealed these names to me for the first time. Now here I was, holding these precious girls in my arms. It was absolutely overwhelming.

Josiah had never lived with his sisters, but had visited them at the foster home regularly. They were in two different houses because of their ages. He knew the babies very well and he could even tell them apart. He loved to hug and kiss them and looked them right in the eyes when talking to them. The girls would light up with smiles and giggles every time they saw him. We are forever grateful that we were chosen to be their new forever family, ensuring they will never be separated again. We are blessed more than we deserve!

All three of our babies adjusted so well to us. They were laughing, babbling, happy, and acting as if they had been ours all along. They talked and watched each other constantly. When we went to eat they grabbed at food every chance they got. They were very observant and curious about everything. Our children were absolutely beautiful!

For the second time, we were faced with some serious health issues with our babies. They all had giardia and ringworm; the twinettes had a really bad case of scabies, and Josiah had molluscum. We came prepared with medication and started their treatments right away. However, there was one issue that we had no control of and could only trust the Lord for His plan. Josiah tested negative for HIV, but the twinettes did not. Since their birth mother was HIV positive, they were born with the HIV virus in their antibodies. We wouldn't know for sure if their bodies were free of the virus until they were about eighteen months old. Just like when we adopted the twin boys, we knew they were divinely appointed to be ours, and the Lord would equip us to handle whatever medical issues they had—this time was no different. When we got home, we were back in the baby zone with diaper bags, bottles, snugglies and lots of potty stops, as we regularly visited Duke Hospital, this time for the twinettes. On their eighteen-month check-up it was determined that they were negative for HIV. We never dreamed this was how our middle-aged season of life would play out, but we were sure it was from the Lord.

I am amazed at how the Lord gives us the gift of love in adoption. When we first began the adoption journey, I was afraid that I would not love my adopted children the same as my biological ones. But the Lord is so faithful. He is the giver of life and love and there is absolutely no difference. I love them all indescribably. In fact, a few days after we arrived home, my girlfriend Theresa Haven came to visit and asked my mom how she liked her new grandchildren. She replied, "You know, I love all of my grandchildren very much. I am very blessed. But I have to say, I think I love all of my adopted grandchildren even more. I am more appreciative because I have seen so many miracles in their lives, with all the health issues and what it took to get them here. When I think of where they might be today if my daughter and Jerry did not go rescue them, it just fills my heart with gratitude. I never expected to be experiencing this in my life. It is just wonderful!"

We had the privilege of spending Thanksgiving Day meeting our birth mother. I had prayed for many hours about this moment, and felt the presence of the Lord so strongly with me. As she walked into the room, radiantly beautiful with a red scarf around her shoulders, she kept her head down and tears were streaming down her face. Then she greeted and kissed her three beautiful babies. Josiah Abel ran to her and she held him in her arms, and then he sat on her lap.

I was shaking and noticed she was too. We were all in tears. I had prepared a letter to her and gave it to the social worker, Yibra, to translate and read aloud. I knew this was going to be a very difficult moment. I wanted to convey sincere love and to encourage her in the Lord. The social worker read through the letter first, and then looked up with tear-filled eyes and said, "Wow, this is absolutely beautiful!"

She translated the letter to my sweet T., who was sitting right beside me. I was literally sitting on the floor at her feet, stroking her arms and her face as she wiped the tears from her eyes with her red scarf. Several times she broke down and Yibra waited to continue with the letter. T. did not look at me, only at the floor. With the permission of everyone involved, there were cameras rolling, to capture this moment for our children to see when they are older. The presence of the Lord was with us and the love in the room was contagious. In my letter I explained how God had orchestrated miracles, and told her the testimony of how He used their names to bring us to this day. I told her how much we loved her and would teach our children about how much she loved and cared for them. We thanked her for giving life to them and assured her we would love and care for them, and teach them about the God who created them. When Yibra finished reading, she said, "Look at her, her countenance has changed."

T. had a smile on her face, her tears were gone, and she stood up, kissed me and said, "Thank you very much; I am so happy now because I see that you love God and that my children are in the hands of God." She even giggled, as we hugged and kissed several more times. Then we proceeded to go over four pages of questions

I had written from the perspective of what the children may ask me when they are older. There were questions about family heritage and personal things like what her favorite color is. I told her I wanted the children to know about her and that she personally gave me the information. She was very cooperative. We also told her about our personal family history and stories, and she was so happy to learn about us. It was truly a divine and intimate time.

We spent three hours together, crying and laughing and getting to know each other. You could sense the power of love and joy in the room. We presented her with several special gifts as a token of our love. There were soft pink pajamas and a beautiful matching robe and slippers, to represent our love being wrapped around her on those cold nights in Addis. Next was a sterling silver necklace with a cross in a circle that says "Faith." This was to remind her that God loves her and has a plan for her and "our" children. Then there was a new purse with toiletries, nail polish, lipstick, pretty smelling lotions, and a beautiful floral umbrella for the rainy season. But the most precious gift of all was made by some of my dear sisters in Christ, Kristi Fields and Debbie Meredith. They handcrafted a beautiful "Prayer Quilt," and infused the referral photos of all three children onto the fabric of the quilt. There were ribbons tied into knots all over it, representing prayers that were said on her behalf. This quilt was passed around to several women's Bible studies, who specifically prayed for her and the children. It was bathed in love and prayers. When I held it up for her to see, she broke down in tears again. It was just beautiful to see her overflowing with a sense of awe that the Lord cared so much for her. Unknowingly, everything was themed in pink, her favorite color. Isn't that just like the Lord, to be concerned about the smallest details of our lives?

After she opened all of her gifts, she said, "Because of meeting you today, hearing this entire story and seeing how much God has been involved, I will never worry again about my children. I have more faith in God than I have ever had in my life. I see Him so clearly and now I know He will take care of my children and me. I thank you with all of my heart. This has turned out even better than I could have ever dreamed or hoped for. I thank God my children have such a good mother, father and family who love God and will love them. You are more than I dreamed for them. I never expected this!"

She was now looking me right in the eyes, instead of at the floor. We kissed, hugged and cried in each other's arms. We felt the Spirit of the Lord with us and I fell in love with her. I honestly feel like she is another daughter to me. She asked if we could keep in touch and write letters and we agreed. We even made arrangements to meet with her later that week to make copies of photos of their birth father who had died, and to give her copies of photos of this amazing day. We started this day as two strangers from opposite sides of the world. We ended as family united in love through Jesus Christ. Josiah Abel, Keziah Selam and Keren Fikir are doubly blessed to have two mothers that love them with all of their hearts.

Thanksgiving Day, November 22, 2007, would go down in history as my absolute favorite. My heart was overflowing with joy and abundant gratitude for having been blessed with my newest daughter T. and our three precious babies. It was a glorious and amazing day!

Our social worker had known T. from the first day she walked into the office, and said this was the absolute best "birth mother meeting" she had ever witnessed. She wanted to use it as a model and tool for future adoptions. She said it felt like she had just attended a class and learned many things. She was in awe of the amazing transformation as she saw T. filled with peace, joy, love, and happiness, which she had never seen in her before.

After our meeting, we went to the Sheraton Hotel for a traditional American Thanksgiving dinner with Bill and Michelle McConomy, all of our children, and the Gladney American staff. It was truly a celebration of gratitude for all the Lord had done!

13 The Forgotten Boys of Kolfe Orphanage

"And even the very hairs of your head are all numbered. So don't be afraid; you are worth more than many sparrows" (Matthew 10:30-31).

Saturday, November 24, 2007, was designated to be a day of rest that we really needed. We were experiencing an emotional roller coaster ride of a lifetime. It was overwhelming to see so many orphanages and extreme poverty. We had breakfast at the hotel and planned to spend the morning playing with the kids. For the first time in his life, Josiah went swimming in the pool. The pool at the Hilton is filled by hot spring water. He had no fear and took to it like a fish. He was jumping in and did not want anyone to get in his way. I realized it was time to start being parents and teach him about healthy boundaries and trust. I told Jerry and Ellie not to catch him right away when he jumped in, so he would realize he could not swim without them. After about three times, he caught on that the pool was a lot bigger than him, and he decided he liked to be caught after all. We also played on the playground and put the kids on swings for their first time. It was delightful!

We met our Gladney staff, Ryan, Travis, Joanna, Avery, and Silas for lunch at the Top View Restaurant where we overlooked the city. It reminded me of Los Angeles, with the buildings in the backdrop of scattered houses on rolling hills, and palm trees swaying in the warm breeze. Travis and Joanna were new employees of Gladney that had arrived the same week. We were their first adoption family experience. Ryan informed us he planned to take us to the Kolfe Boys Orphanage after lunch, where 180 boys, ranging from ages ten to twenty years old, lived.

While we were waiting to come to Ethiopia, Ellie had asked Mary T. for a humanitarian aid project she could work on. Mary sent us a list of many needs, and Ellie picked the project of raising funds to build a library at the Kolfe Boys Orphanage. She was able to raise $1,200 with the help and support of my friend Jennifer Hoffert and the Franklin Academy Charter School in Wake Forest, North Carolina. We never realized we would actually visit there.

As we were eating lunch, I started to think about Ryan's plans. I started to contemplate the wisdom of taking our beautiful fourteen-year-old daughter to a compound of 180 testosterone-filled boys, and decided it was not a good idea. So I suggested we go shopping, instead of visiting the orphanage. I explained we had $250 and we planned to buy a small gift for all the families that had helped finance our adoption. This was going to bless the Ethiopian economy as well. He shook his head no, and explained we were going to Kolfe. I looked at him with a serious face and hoped he could read my mind. I was not at all interested in visiting the boys' orphanage! I even talked to Jerry and asked him to make another suggestion. But Ryan had a plan.

As he would have it, we began the forty-five minute trek to Kolfe, and I prayed all the way there for God to thwart Ryan's plans. I asked God for a flat tire, or a small fender bender or whatever He could do to get us off the road to Kolfe. Please, Lord, not Kolfe!

When we turned the corner and began to slow down, I started to shake inside. I had a strong sense that something was going to happen there. Suddenly, there it was; it looked like a concentration camp from the Nazi era. It was surrounded with barbed wire and fencing, with a guard tower overlooking the fence. The guard at the gate looked at us, as the driver beeped his horn to gain entrance. He opened the gate and we began the next adventure.

Jerry and I told Ellie to stand between us when we got out of the car, making a hedge of protection around her. I had a baby in a snuggly, Ellie had a baby in a snuggly, and Jerry had Josiah Abel. I told her to stand closely between us and hoped we would stay for fifteen minutes and get out of there.

As I looked up, the first thing I noticed was all the boys running toward the car to greet us with big white smiles and happy faces.

They were well-groomed and were shouting in English, "Hello, Hello!"—so excited to have visitors. I opened the car door and as my foot touched the soil, I heard God whisper in my ear, *"I brought you here for a reason. I know how many hairs are on every one of their heads. Tell them I have not forgotten them. Tell them to seek Me and they will find Me. I brought you here to give them a Mama's hug."* I started to cry and was overwhelmed as I got out of the car. It is always overwhelming when I hear that whisper that takes me by total surprise. I was trying to swallow my tears and stuff my emotions down, because I didn't want anyone to see me crying.

The boys surrounded us and were yelling out their names as they introduced themselves. They were explaining the meaning of their names and the biblical reference to it. I was so surprised that they were so friendly, clean, and spoke English. I was expecting the worst, of course. They asked if we would like to tour their compound, as Ryan started to lead us in. As we walked, I had to hold on because the ground was so broken up with holes, rocks, and puddles everywhere. Two boys were literally holding my arms and guiding me. I was afraid of twisting my ankles and falling down with the baby.

Within a few minutes, the fear was gone and a sense of peace was bathed over me. I was falling in love with these precious boys. They were very polite and hospitable, asking lots of questions about us, our adoption and about America. They pointed out each building and told us where they lived, with pride and excitement. The windows were broken throughout the compound, and it looked like it hadn't been maintained in at least twenty years. Addis Ababa is the highest elevation in Ethiopia and it gets very cold at night. We were staying at the Hilton, with blankets and several layers of clothing, and I was still freezing every night. As I looked at the broken windows in their dorms, my mind was focused on the fact that they must really freeze at night. The beds were metal bunks that also looked over twenty years old. The mattress pads were deteriorated and the blankets were thin and torn.

My heart was breaking as I heard that whisper say, *"Don't let them see you cry or look sad. Smile and be happy with them. I brought you here for a reason. Trust Me."* I was trying to force a smile so much that my face was hurting. They had such a sense of pride, and I was complimenting them on the neatness of their rooms and anything I could think of. There were flowers and a garden planted in among the rocks and I told them how pretty they looked. They took us to watch the boys playing soccer in the field full of rocks and holes. They were running and playing with joy and laughter, in spite of their horrible living conditions. The goal was two poles, with flying strings that used to be nets, blowing in the breeze. The boys made two teams, while the rest cheered on the side lines. After two goals were scored, a new group of boys would run on the field to replace the losing team. This way they all got a chance to play. They wore regular clothes and shoes or sandals. Their ball was old and tattered, but they didn't seem to notice.

This place was so neglected and depressing, yet there was a spirit of joy that was contagious. I suddenly realized at one point, Ellie was at the far side of the field from where we were, surrounded by boys laughing and talking. Jerry and I are very protective over our children and would never put any of them in a dangerous situation. This is why I didn't even want to visit Kolfe. But it was evident that the boys were no danger. I told them that Ellie had raised money, 11,000 birr, to fund their soon-to-be-built library. The boys were so surprised that a young girl was able to accomplish such a great task. They thanked her and bowed their heads with respect to her. As I began asking them questions, they expressed interest in becoming doctors, teachers, carpenters, and going to America. They had dreams, goals and aspirations of being a positive influence and contributors to their society. They talked about school and said they only played soccer on weekends, because during the week they must study. As we walked this compound and talked with the boys, I knew I could never forget them and that I had to do something. I knew I was never going to be the same again, but I had no idea how much of an impact this really had in my life.

As we were walking toward the car, the boys knew we were getting ready to leave. One of them, Tesfa, said to me, "Can you help us? Our government has no money and they have not maintained this compound in over thirty years. Some people have started to visit and take pictures. But they don't come back and no one knows we are here. No one helps us, they forgot about us." He spoke in a soft voice with a matter-of-fact attitude. He was not angry or resentful.

He was honestly and gently pleading on behalf of all the boys there.

Suddenly, it was as if the Holy Spirit spoke through me as I answered him, saying, "I will go back to America. I will tell God's people about you. And if they will listen to Him, they will start to visit and they will help you. But remember, when you start to see more Americans coming here to help you, remember it is GOD sending them to you, not me. He has not forgotten you!" The boys teared up and smiled, and asked us to please come back to visit again.

It was getting dark and it was time to leave. As I walked toward the car I heard the whisper, *I brought you here to give them a Mama's hug. Tell them I have not forgotten them. I know how many hairs are on each of their heads. I have a plan for them. Tell them to seek after Me and they will find Me.*" I looked over at Jerry and said, "We can't leave yet. God just told me I have to hug all the boys." Jerry looked back at me wide-eyed and said, "YOU CAN'T DO THAT! It's getting dark, the driver has to go, and we have to leave now." I gave him that look and said, "Jerry, God said I have to!" Since he has experienced this many times before, he shrugged his shoulders, huffed and puffed, and walked over to Ryan to tell him that I had to hug all the boys. I shouted for all the boys to line up in front of me as I stood with my arms wide open.

They began to giggle and looked at Ryan like, "Is she serious?" He shouted to the boys, "This is MAMA Eileen, it is OK. Line up quickly." The boys lined up, giggly and nervous, looking at each other with surprise.

As I reached out to them I was fully expecting them to be stiff and hesitant to get my hug. But God did something. As I hugged and kissed the cheeks of each one of them, they leaned in and melted into my arms. I put my hand on each head and told them God knew how many hairs were on their heads, and He sent me all the way from America to give them a Mama's hug and kiss. I still had a baby in the snuggly on my chest, so she got lots of hugs too. Many of them were in tears and squeezed me tightly. I didn't let go until I had a good long hug. One boy cried as he told me he hadn't been hugged like that since his mama died. Another said, "I always wondered what it felt like to get a Mama's hug."

I didn't realize it at the time, but Jerry, Ellie, and Ryan were on the sidelines, watching and weeping. Little Josiah was laughing as he watched, and he started kissing Jerry's cheek repeatedly, as to mimic me. Some of the boys went running to other parts of the compound, bringing new boys to the line. Several got in the line a second time. Even the older boys were waiting for their Mama hug. I stood there and waited until it was obvious that there were no more boys waiting. I felt like I was standing on holy ground. One of the older boys came and held my hand tightly, as he rattled off a conversation in Amharic. When I asked Habtamu, the young man who had spoken English during our tour, to translate for me, he said, "He is asking you not to forget about us and to help him get out of here." With that, I began to cry and got in the car to leave. What an emotional day. I cried all the way home and all through the night. I could not sleep.

I wrote a post on our blog that evening and this was my prayer: "God, help me to help these forgotten boys of Kolfe. My heart and mind have been transformed to understand James 1:27 in a new way. Pure religion is to care for orphans and widows in their distress. This does not just mean adoption, but caring for all the kids in the orphanages as well. Help me to find a way to help Kolfe and start a campaign when we get home. I pray my heavenly Father will go before me and prepare the hearts of those who will join me and be blessed beyond all measure.

"I know many people are opening their hearts to orphan care and adoption. People will adopt babies, especially girls, because they know they are rescuing them from a life of probable prostitution. But who will speak for the boys, the future leaders and fathers and husbands of the next generation? I never thought about the older boys at all. Forgive me, Father, I am the guiltiest. I didn't even want to go visit them! Thank you, God for the experience You blessed me with today. Please help me to make a difference now!"

After this experience, we decided to give the cash we had designated to pay our hotel bill to Gladney to purchase new blankets and mattresses for Kolfe. We charged the hotel bill to our credit card. Because it is a government-run orphanage, there is a lot of paperwork involved in making a purchase so big, and it takes time. Then we bought ten soccer balls and pumps and headed back for another visit with the boys the next day. They were shocked to see us return so soon. We spent several more hours talking with them and took lots of photos and video. We planned to put it on our blog when we got home. As we were leaving the second time, I wrote my name and e-mail on a piece of paper and handed it to Bantamlak, saying, "Let's become pen pals. Write to me sometime and I will write back." We got in the car to leave, tears streaming down my face, and I knew I was not the same person leaving Kolfe as when I arrived. But I had no idea what the Lord still had coming!

14 Trials Begin

Consider it pure joy, my brothers, whenever you face trials of many kinds, because you know that the testing of your faith develops perseverance. Perseverance must finish its work so that you may be mature and complete, not lacking anything. If any of you lacks wisdom, he should ask God, who gives generously to all without finding fault, and it will be given to him. But when he asks, he must believe and not doubt, ... (James 1:2-6).

We arrived home at Raleigh Durham Airport on Wednesday, November 28, 2007 to a wonderful reception of family and friends with balloons and banners. It was so good to be home and to hold all my other babies too. We were exhausted physically, emotionally, and spiritually. Our lives would never be the same after all we had experienced in Ethiopia. Lots of friends and family came bearing gifts and congratulations, as well as delivering meals for the next month. We are so blessed to have so many loving people in our lives.

The day after we got home, Keziah started to run a fever, her neck swelled and was tender to the touch. My pediatrician sent us to the ER for blood tests and a CT scan. At 2:00 a.m. the baby was admitted, due to the unknowns about her possible exposure to diseases. She had an undiagnosable infection, so they gave her IV antibiotics. I held her in my arms for two days as the antibiotic proved effective. We were sent home and continued to give her antibiotics six times per day. The doctor said if the swelling started back, to immediately return to the hospital. They were concerned the swelling could block her airway, so we could not delay. We had to watch her like a hawk for twenty-four hours a day.

While I was at the hospital, Jerry took all the other kids to the doctor and they were all sick with a cold, cough, and ear infections. The prescriptions cost more than $600 and were not covered by insurance. Our house became an infirmary overnight.

Praise the Lord, Keziah was healed by the third day. Jerry packed up our fifteen passenger van named "Larry Boy, the Big Green Pickle," with all the kids in all the new car seats to pick us up at the hospital. Then at 1:30 p.m., my son Jonathan called and said, "Mom, we won't be there to pick you up for a little while longer. We were on our way and we just got in a car accident. All the traffic in front of us came to a stop and the truck behind plowed into us. We are all okay, but Miss Ruby, our dog, got a bump or two. The back of the van was dented, but the doors still open." Thank the Lord, everyone was okay.

When we finally got home, the house was a mess, with unpacked suitcases and about twenty loads of laundry waiting for me. Then we discovered that the washing machine had broken and would cost more to fix than it was worth. So we headed out to buy a new one. This was not in the budget!

Melissa was five months pregnant and helping so much with the kids. Then she got sick with the cold and cough too. Randy was a trouper, helping with everything, and he even delivered food to me at the hospital.

Then Jonathan's truck broke down and had to go to the shop for major repairs.

When Jerry went back to work, his boss informed him that he was not going to be paid for the two weeks we were in Ethiopia. This was a shock!

My dad came down with pneumonia and was very sick.

Christmas was just a few weeks away and we were all sick and exhausted.

I was talking with the Lord, asking Him why these things were happening. I asked what He was teaching me in this and here is what I got: "Do you still love Me, even when things are hard?"

I have learned that many times we have the mountaintop experiences with God and then BAM! Things take another turn and we hit the pit. There are many false doctrines teaching prosperity in our culture. They say if you do things right, there should be no difficulties or problems in your life. But the Scriptures teach us differently.

"My grace is sufficient for you, for my power is made perfect in weakness" (2 Corinthians 12:9).

As I was reflecting, I remembered the Lord began this journey with the book of Job, chapter 42. I was feeling a bit like Job, with the pressures and trials of life crashing down around me. Then I literally had to laugh. We have to keep a sense of humor and "choose joy" in the midst of the trials. We cannot allow Satan to rob us of the joy that is abundantly flowing through the Spirit's power. Life is hard; it is not easy, but we can do all things through Christ who strengthens us.

The book of James tells us to consider it pure joy *"whenever"* we face trial of many kinds, because the testing of our faith develops perseverance. Perseverance must finish its work so that we may be mature and complete, not lacking anything. There is a guarantee that we will have trials, so we shouldn't be surprised or discouraged. We must always remind each other that He will never leave or forsake us, and He promises to give us wisdom, help, and hope as believers in Jesus Christ. I am overwhelmed with love, joy, peace, and hope that are the blessings He gives when we know His Word and trust Him alone! Trials are often so much more than I can handle, which is why I bow my knees in prayer and cry out to my Abba Father. I can testify He is faithful to always carry me through to the other side.

The LORD gives strength to his people; the Lord blesses his people with peace (Psalm 29:11).

15 A Voice for the Orphan

We were finally feeling better and I started to post on our blog again. While we were in Ethiopia, I had no idea the Lord had already started stirring the hearts of people at home. After reading my post about the forgotten boys of Kolfe, Jerry's sister Maria was compelled to organize a fund-raiser, January 6, 2008, at the Caffé Opera in Monrovia, California. Her daughter Jaclyn is an accomplished opera singer and was going to perform a concert to benefit Kolfe. This was just weeks after we got home. I was even more flabbergasted when she called to tell us she had already sold eighty tickets at $100 each, and that we were the keynote speakers and had to be there.

We were still suffering from jet lag, getting over illness, and I now had five children under five years old—two in diapers— who were totally dependent on me all day long. We had three babies adjusting to their new life. Christmas was just over and all the decorations had to be taken down. There was so much to do. We were having major attacks on our finances and it just seemed impossible. I didn't have time to prepare a presentation to speak at a fund-raiser. There was no way we could just pick up and go to California; this was more than I could handle; in fact, it was insane! But I knew I had to go to the Lord in prayer. He seemed to be doing something and I had to consult Him about it.

After praying and talking about it, we realized Jerry's job required him to spend one week a month in California, so he could schedule it for that week. He had accumulated enough airline miles to pay for my plane ticket and we would have free accommodations with family and friends. Melissa, Randy, my parents, Jonathan, and Ellie said they would hold down the fort, and were in full support of us attending this fund-raiser. It was only going to be for the weekend and everything seemed to be taken care of. As I prayed, the Lord gave me complete peace that we were to go and He was obviously in control.

On Friday, January 4, 2008, we were on a nonstop flight to California, using the flight time to work on the presentation for the fund-raiser. Jerry got the window seat and I was in the middle seat, which meant I was going to be sitting really close to the man next to me for the next five hours. I politely greeted him right away. "Hello, it looks like we are going to be neighbors for awhile, welcome to the neighborhood. My name is Eileen." We exchanged quick answers as to why we were going to LA. He started asking more questions, and I suggested he read the printout from my blog, telling the story of our adoption and trip to Ethiopia, so that I could get to work. He attentively began reading while we were engrossed in our preparations.

When he finished, he literally started to cry. He handed me the paper, wiping his eyes, and said, "Now I know why I am in this seat. I travel all the time and have never experienced anything like this. I am a producer of documentary films and I am going to help you with your presentation." He stood up, reached into the overhead compartment to retrieve his computer and said, "Okay, guys, let's get to work!" He was so excited and genuinely moved by our story. We worked the entire flight, and before we knew it, it was time to land. Then he said, "I know this is crazy, but I think God is telling me I am supposed to come to your fund-raiser and video everything. Give me all the information and I am going to rearrange my schedule to be there." To our surprise, he showed up and made a mini-documentary. Then several weeks later, he called to tell us he was working on the final proof with his business partner, who was personal friends with the producer of the Oprah Winfrey show. They were submitting it for the show's review. We were very surprised.

The fund-raiser was an absolute success. There were many hearts touched and they got a good dose of the gospel as well. A friend of Maria's, who could not attend, promised to match the highest donation received, which was $1,700. Several people pledged to talk to other friends and coworkers, and raised an additional $1,000. My brothers-in-law, Jeff and Jim, made a gift for all the attendees. A CD of Jaclyn's amazing performance was recorded by

Jim; and the cover of the CD, produced by Jeff, was comprised of artwork and photos of the Kolfe boys. It was absolutely beautiful!

A check was sent to the Gladney Humanitarian Aid department, for $8,000. I wrote to Gladney and Ryan in Ethiopia, explaining that God had started a ministry for us to help the boys at the Kolfe Orphanage, and this money was to be designated specifically for the projects Ryan had said he wanted to complete when we were there.

Ryan Brown and his wife, Abby, worked for the Gladney Adoption agency in Ethiopia. Their job was to process all the paperwork to get orphans approved for adoption, and then to match the families with a child. However, Ryan's heart was too big to focus on that alone. He decided to bring families to visit the Kolfe Boys Orphanage, even though he knew the odds of anyone wanting to adopt an older boy were slim. He hoped as people saw the needs of these boys they would be inspired to help them, and maybe even consider adopting one of them. Ryan started a humanitarian aid branch of ministry for Gladney and the Kolfe Orphanage became our project. He wanted to repair the windows, plumbing, and kitchen. He had dreams to renovate this orphanage, and it was going to take a lot of money, but he also knew God was able.

We started posting on our blog and the Lord used it to inspire many people to get involved. We began to hear from people telling us they now had the faith to pursue adoption after watching our journey. Others were sending money for Kolfe, and within two months of being home, we heard from Gladney that more than $50,000 had come in specifically for the Kolfe Orphanage. They were the forgotten boys no more. The word spread to people from all over the country, who began visiting the boys as they traveled for their adoptions. These are two letters I received from Ryan:

Hey Eileen,

Glad to hear things are going well. I went back to Kolfe to let them know you had left money for blankets and the older guys all said they didn't need blankets, and decided the money would be best spent on shoes for the young boys. I thought it was pretty sweet that they wanted to spend the money on the younger guys. I hope you are okay with the money being spent that way, let me know if you are not okay with it. Also, about the fund-raiser ... there is a plumbing problem that needs to be fixed. The pipes from 2 bathrooms are leaking, and the sewage is seeping up through the ground. I would like this to be the next project, so could we use some of the money from the fund-raiser to repair this problem? The boys at Kolfe and I are truly grateful that you did not forget what you saw or how it made you feel.

Ryan

A few weeks later this came:

Eileen,

Thanks for all the great news. You (Okay, God really, but using you) have done such an amazing job sharing about the guys at Kolfe and I couldn't be more grateful. One of the families told me they will be sending a check for $25,000 to Gladney to help with renovations at Kolfe, and a friend who came to adopt earlier let me know that he and a friend will be sending in a check for $10,000 for renovations at Kolfe. Things are happening too fast! Thank you for keeping me up to date with all God is doing through those willing to be used.

Ryan

I received another letter saying he was getting so many requests to take people who were adopting through different agencies to visit Kolfe, that it was turning into a full-time job. All of this activity did create a full-time job for Gladney to hire an Ethiopian man to handle the humanitarian aid and Kolfe projects.

Just as the Holy Spirit had prompted me to tell the boys when I was there, they were now seeing God's people visit and help them. The Kolfe Orphanage has been completely renovated and looks nothing like it did in 2007, and several of the boys have also been adopted. We serve an amazing God!

16 Journey to Solomon

In addition to taking care of and adjusting to our new family, homeschooling, cooking, cleaning, laundry, shopping, doing life, speaking engagements, and the Kolfe ministry, another interesting thing happened. I had given the Kolfe boys my e-mail address and suggested they write to me. Two weeks after we got home, I was shocked to receive a letter from "Solomon." When I saw his name I remembered exactly who he was. As we had toured the compound of Kolfe there was one boy walking with us that stood out in the crowd. He was a handsome young man with a small and skinny stature. The sadness on his face and in his eyes was radiant. When I tried to make eye contact with him, he looked down at the ground and started kicking rocks. He was shy and looked so sad and lonely. It was as if he was telling me, "Nobody cares about me and I have no purpose in life." I still have a vivid memory of watching him walk beside me as we toured the compound. He spoke very little English, but he was communicating with his body language and facial expressions. He posed in some photos with us, so I had his picture to look at when we got home.

After he began e-mailing me, I realized when I was in Ethiopia I never saw a computer. The hotel had Internet service, but it was slow and expensive. I asked Solomon how he was able to e-mail me. He said the government gave him money for transportation to school, and he started walking every day so that he could use the money for the Internet café. He also said he had never even touched a computer until he got my e-mail address. He asked a friend of his at school to teach him how to make an e-mail account and how to use the computer. He said when I hugged and kissed all of the boys that day at Kolfe, he knew there was something very different about me. He wanted to write and see if I would write back to him as I said I would.

I now felt an enormous responsibility to respond to his e-mails immediately, because of his great sacrifice. I couldn't believe the great lengths he went to just to write to me. I knew he was all alone in that orphanage, reaching across the world for someone to show him love and give him time and attention. He was all alone in this world with not one living relative. I knew his living conditions and that he was hungry most of the time too. I didn't understand why God was putting this responsibility in my life as well! As I read Solomon's letters, I would cry and my heart would break a little more with every word. At times, I honestly felt like this was more than I could handle.

One day I felt the Lord impress upon me to post his letters on the blog. With Solomon's permission, I started posting his letters; because I realized, though we are called to care for orphans, most people in the USA do not have the opportunity to really know and visit them. Solomon became the face and name to the orphan, and his letters revealed the heart cry of the orphan for the world to hear. These are some of the first letters I received from him:

"Hi Eileen I am Solomon. I am reading your pleasurable email letter. I am really happy about that thank you for everything. Eileen be for you come to us i did not know any one out of the campus when something happened to me may be it is hard or not i a am trying to solve by myself but now i am very lucky because i get you. When you take me permission i want to call you my mum. Eileen my mother was dead when i was one years old. I am the only child for my mum but i am not lucky to saw her but God never forgot me he take me you. I would like to reading a bible before i sleep because i understand how God loves me very much not only me he loves all human beings. Eileen i told to Habtamu to writing for you. He says writing soon. Mum after i will write other letter for you God blessing all of you."

I told Solomon I would be honored and privileged to be his MUM. I asked him to tell me more about his childhood, because I wanted to grow our relationship. I wanted to help him, but had no idea how.

"Hello my dear mum. I was writing for you for my mother

today. I am writing for you about my life when i was childhood. Mum after my mother died my father take the responsibility to protect me and he challenged many problems because of me he treated me like a mother and father. Always he tried to happy me. He told me that study hard but i don't know why always he told me this in that time. I remember when i was 8 years old i was asked him why always say to me study hard. He told me always this because of one thing when something happened to me one day how you can lead your life you know that we are poor therefore the only chance to live a better life for future is when you study hard. I understand everything that time we are not any man to help us. After two years later, when i was ten years old one day at 1:00 pm my father is very sick the next day he goes to clinic and get medical care the doctors are trying to save his life but they can't. When the doctors told me that i can't control myself i am really sad because i lose one man i have. After he died i was alone. After two weeks one man he knows my father came to me and i told him everything after that he finished all process to bring to me orphan campus finally i came the campus when i was 10 years old. I have been lived in this campus for 6 years now. Shortly my history like this. Mum i don't have computer access. I am sending you the message by using computer center services. When i used the computer to 1 minute i pay 20 cents, 1 hour 12 birr. It is very difficult to me but i promise i write for you two or three times in a week. Mum Mike and his son are coming today to us. I meet with them. They also visit the library give for us candy pen and candy also ball. I am really enjoyed with them. Mum i think about you i can't tolerate your love."

"I MISSED YOU SO MUCH. I pray to God to meet with you mum. GOD BLESS YOU FOREVER MUM."

"Hello my dear mum Eileen. mum i haven't a job. I am studying marketing in a diploma program I am scored high mark in the first year 94 out of 100 now i am learning 2nd year. The campus are giving for me 20 birr in a month for transportation purpose but my college is not far so i used that money to writing for you. Mum my future plan is after i will graduate when i will get any kinds of job i want to work and to help poor peoples but in Ethiopia is not easy to get a job when you need to open new business the atmosphere is not good because the taxes are very heavy, the inflation rate are increasing day-today because of this many Ethiopian are unemployment. Mum after i saw you my dream is to live with you because you are different to others, your smile, advise, generous, respect are attract me. I haven't mothers get mothers love so i am sure i get that love for you also i haven't sister i get the sister and dad. You know Eileen how much happy when i am get all this but mum when it is difficult don't worry. Mum i won't to writing for you day to day but 20 birr is not adequate so when you send me some money i contact with you day to day and also send me a bible. I have a bible but i need the English one. Thank you for everything mum. I would like to say HAPPY X-MAS for you, dad and sister. God bless you forever mum."

Solomon and I wrote regularly for the next two years. We fell in love and decided God had made us a family. The government regulations deemed him too old to be adopted legally, but in our hearts we were family now. I sent him a Bible and little care packages, with money for the Internet and to buy clothes. We sent him his first birthday gift in his life. My main goal in this relationship was to disciple him in the Lord and the Holy Scriptures. I encouraged him to read his Bible and to pray for the Lord to show Himself real in his life. God had a great plan for his life and Solomon should seek Him for advice in everything. I would share things that I was learning as I studied the Scriptures, and tell him about life in the crazy Mestas' house.

In Ethiopia, all students take a national exam in the tenth grade. If they do not pass, the government considers them to be disqualified from any additional educational investment. They are not permitted to go to any government state-funded high school or university, and they can no longer live in the orphanage. The students' only hope is to get into a private school, but that cost money. Solomon had failed the national exam just before we met him, and was destined to be homeless and without an education. The Director of the orphanage, Johannes, asked some private schools in the area for a scholarship. One school, the Infonet College, responded with one scholarship and he gave it to Solomon. He was assigned to the marketing program and told me all the time that he was studying hard to pass his classes.

One day, Solomon said the school was having financial difficulty and was not going to be able to continue his scholarship.

Several weeks later, I woke up feeling a burden to send him some money. I had received a donation through the blog and I contacted Gladney to help me get it to him with a traveling adoptive family. It was hand-delivered to Solomon. A few days later he said, "Mom, you sent the exact amount of money I needed for school. The director told me that if I didn't pay the full tuition by Friday I had to leave the school. The money got to me just in time and it was the exact amount." I had no idea!

In May 2009, he wrote that he was going to graduate in August 2009 and asked me to please come to his graduation. My heart broke as I explained that it was impossible. We had no money and I had so many responsibilities at home. Africa is not a weekend trip! But I told him I would talk to God about it. Lord knows, this was really going to take a miracle!

Ellie has spent every summer for the last four years serving in orphanages around the world. This is her passion. She was in Guatemala working at the Agua Viva Orphanage, and when I picked her up at the airport she immediately said, "Mama, I think God spoke to me about you going to Solomon's graduation." I was surprised that this was the first thing she mentioned, instead of telling us all about her trip. She said one night the Director of her orphanage shared his testimony. He was raised in that same orphanage and an American lady started to sponsor and write to him. When he graduated high school, she came all the way from America to attend his graduation ceremony. He talked about what an impact that had on his life, the other kids, and the village. People could not believe that an American would come all that way for an orphan boy. He became a born-again believer because of her mentorship, and was now getting ready to go to Seminary in Tennessee to be a pastor.

We were in tears as she shared this story and then she said, "Mama, this is the story of you and Solomon and you have to go to his graduation." I started to chuckle and said, "Did God tell you where I'm going to get the money and time to leave all the 'littles' too?" The trip would cost at least $3,000 and I would have to stay for at least a week. And I didn't want to go alone. My heart was racing and I felt like this was just too much for me to handle. There was just no way this could be possible. After our dinner discussion that evening, we all agreed as a family to pray for another miracle.

I posted about the situation on our blog to ask for wisdom and prayer. Would you believe, within days, people I didn't even know started sending letters with money telling me I had to go to his graduation? Within a few weeks of posting it, I had $3,000 to pay for the trip and not a penny more. God was in control and showing me again, He had a plan!

I couldn't believe this was really happening. I prayed for wisdom and heard Him whisper, *"Someone is going with you to take photos and video."* I had no idea who that was going to be or why photos and video were specified. I posted it on the blog but didn't hear from anyone. Jerry couldn't take time off from work and Ellie was going to care for the 'littles.' We had no money for another ticket anyway. Jonathan was working and Melissa had a new baby. We were all waiting for God to reveal who this person was.

My cousin Georgie, who lives in New York City, called on a regular basis to talk about his newfound faith in the Lord Jesus Christ. The Lord blessed us with the opportunity to encourage him in the faith, and Jerry actually baptized him the week before we went to get our new babies in Ethiopia. One evening he asked what was new in the crazy Mestas' house, knowing there is never a dull moment around here. I told him the Lord was sending me back to Ethiopia for Solomon's graduation, and He told me someone was coming with me to take photos and video, but had not yet revealed who it was. We kept talking and all of a sudden Georgie said, "Eileen, the weirdest thing just happened to me. I think I just heard God tell me I am supposed to go with you to Ethiopia."

"What?" I responded. "Do you know how to do photography and video?"

"Of course, I have been in the entertainment industry for years, and as a manager this was one of my jobs. This is crazy, this kind of thing happens to you, not me. I really think I heard Him talking to me. But I don't have any money right now. I can't go to Ethiopia!" I told him I didn't have the money either, but I posted it on our blog and within a few weeks the money came in. He had never had to raise funds for anything, but said he had great friends that might help him, and he was going to contact them. He called me two days later to say that within twenty-four hours he had almost $2,000! Do you SEE God? So we started making plans to travel in just a few weeks' time. Ethiopia, here I come again!

Photographs

Our wedding, 1979.   *Melissa, 10 years old; Jonathan,*
3 years old; and Ellie, 4 months.

Our family, 1993. Our last photo as residents of CA.
Time to move to NC to raise our family.

*Jeremiah & James
Gotcha' Day, 2003,
with Dr. McArtor.*

*Holding the twins for
the first time! Get me
the breast pump!
July 9, 2003.*

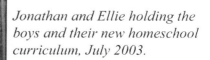

*Jonathan and Ellie holding the
boys and their new homeschool
curriculum, July 2003.*

James (left) and Jeremiah (right), five months old, September 2003.

Grandma and Grandpa, Babe & Betty Farrell, moved in and fell in love. These baby boys gave us all a new lease on life!

Proud Papa and his boys.

Melissa's glorious wedding day. She married Randy on November 17, 2006. The Lord's blessings abound!

And the family grows again!

Josiah Abel referral picture, August 2007.

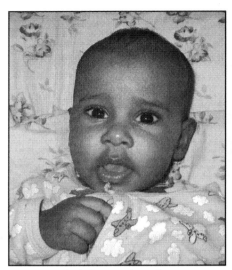

*Keziah Selam referral picture,
August 2007.*

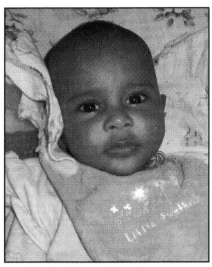

*Keren Fikir referral picture,
August 2007.*

*The Quilt made for
our Birth Mother,
with the children's
referral photos
appliquéd on.
Eileen with Kristi
Fields.*

Meeting Josiah Abel, at the Gladney home in Ethiopia, November 19, 2007.

Our new family, Addis Ababa, Ethiopia.

Thanksgiving in Ethiopia with Bill and Michelle McConomy and their daughter PraiseTinsae, November 2007.

Kolfe Boys Orphanage, Addis Ababa, Ethiopia, November 2007.

Our first tour, with the boys showing us their dorms at Kolfe.

The day we met Solomon at Kolfe Orphanage; our first photo together; 2007.

Solomon's Graduation, 2009!

Proud Mama of the Valedictorian! Solomon's Graduation, Addis Ababa, Ethiopia.

Solomon, Cousin Georgie, and Misganaw; Graduation in Ethiopia, 2009.

A Mama's hug
and sharing the
gospel of Jesus,
Ethiopia 2009.

Kolfe Mama
Eileen in the
middle of the
Kolfe boys.

The
welcoming
committee
for Solomon,
Raleigh, NC,
June 2010!

Solomon is finally in the USA with his Mama!

First family photo with Solomon, at the airport!

The growing Pearce family! Randy, Melissa, Vaden, Callum & Cana, May 2012.

Our family, 2011.

Our beautiful grandchildren, the "Pearcelings," Vaden, Cana & Baby Callum.

The beautiful Pearce Family; our son-in-law Randy and daughter Melissa, holding Callum, with 3-year-old Cana (left) and 4-year-old Vaden (right).

17 Back to Ethiopia

*For we are God's workmanship, created in Christ Jesus
to do good works, which God prepared in advance for us to do
(Ephesians 2:10).*

Georgie and I met at Dulles Airport, Ethiopian Airlines
terminal. I never expected to be back there so soon. We planned
to stay in Addis Ababa for two weeks at the Cherokee House, and
Gladney was letting me hire one of their drivers. I honestly could
not believe this was happening. There I was, Mrs. Homeschool
Mom, with my cousin Georgie, a prominent Manager to the Hip
Hop stars. He is blonde, blue-eyed, short, stocky, and covered from
head to toe with tattoos. I call him Tattoo Man. He has a very strong
New York accent, with a baritone raspy voice like a character from
the *Godfather* movie. We made an interesting pair, to say the least.

We spent twenty hours on the plane talking, laughing, crying,
and reading the Scriptures together. We were both absolutely sure
we were on an assignment from the Lord and felt like we were
treading on holy ground. We both also felt like there was going to
be something special about this trip that was yet to be revealed. I
kept wondering why I was specifically burdened to take video and
photos. Georgie was excited to visit the boys at Kolfe and planned
to buy them a new TV and show them the *Jesus* film. Georgie had
traveled the world in private planes and stayed at five-star hotels,
but he had not yet been to the continent of Africa. He was in for a
surprise.

I noticed people looking at us a lot on the plane, but no one
was friendly like on my last journey to Ethiopia. We met one lady in

the Dulles gateway who said she was going to Ethiopia on business, but she was not very friendly. She was sitting within eyesight on the plane and I noticed her looking at me several times, but as soon as I looked at her, she turned her head. I wanted to visit with her, but I assumed she was antisocial. Before we knew it we were landing in Addis Ababa, Ethiopia again.

Cherokee House made arrangements to pick us up at the airport. My friend Misganaw, who had been an exchange student here in Raleigh through the Cherokee Foundation the year before, was going to bring Solomon from the orphanage to the airport to greet us.

It took several hours to get through customs, and even though we had been writing for almost two years, I was nervous about seeing Solomon again. I kept reminiscing to the last time I had seen him in person. I had hardly talked with him, because he was very shy and didn't speak much English. I was shaking and tears were already filling my eyes. Then suddenly, there he was in the crowd, waving his arms at me with tears streaming down his face as well. It was so surreal. The last time I saw him he had been gazing at me with hopelessness like I had never seen, but this day, he was beaming with joy and excitement. I ran through the gate and we embraced each other like long-lost friends. We held each other and cried, both shaking and in awe that this was really happening.

Brianna, from the Cherokee House, greeted us with a welcome sign and said the new Ethiopian Director for Children's HopeChest was also on our flight and would be joining us. After waiting for another hour, we were surprised to see it was the antisocial lady we had met in Dulles. Her luggage was not on the flight, so she was in customs all that time. When she joined our group she was very surprised to see us there too. As we shook hands with introductions, I told her I had wanted to visit with her on the plane, but she appeared to be a real snob. She burst into laughter and said, "You know, I wanted to talk to you and I couldn't stop looking at you guys on the plane. But you were such an interesting looking couple and I kept trying to figure you out. You didn't look like siblings, or a married couple, but you were way too friendly to be coworkers. It was kind of weird." We all burst into laughter and we agreed we were an interesting pair! She was my roommate for the next two weeks and we had a very nice time together.

Solomon was Georgie's roommate for the next two weeks as well. He only weighed about 90 pounds and stood 5 feet, 3 inches tall. One goal was to fatten him up while we were there. He had never eaten in a restaurant, and had no idea how or what to order from the menu. He had never eaten any of that food, and did not know how to use utensils. In Ethiopia they eat with their fingers, using their national bread, injera, which is like a sourdough sponge cake tortilla. Everything he ate for breakfast, lunch, and dinner the entire two weeks was a first for him.

Our first day there was very interesting for Georgie. He had never been to Africa or seen such extreme poverty before. I tried to prepare him, but there is nothing like seeing it for yourself. Addis Ababa reminds me of California. It is beautifully landscaped, with rolling hills and palm trees, and its architecture reminded me of the 1950s. It was like traveling through several centuries in time all at once. Most of the cars are at least twenty years old, but scattered among the traffic, I saw brand new Hummers, Mercedes, and Toyota Tundra trucks. There were pack mules carrying heavy loads on their backs, and shepherds wearing white robes and turbans, herding sheep in the middle of the roads as well. There were hundreds of children and people begging in the streets.

On our first day, the Cherokee House driver wanted to take us on a tour of Addis Ababa, so we accepted his offer. He had a little blue car that was about thirty years old, and you could see the ground through the floorboards. Georgie was in the front seat and Solomon and I were in the back. This was also his first time to get a tour of his own city. We had been driving for about an hour and I noticed Georgie didn't look good. He was very quiet, his face was turning pale and his head was swaying back and forth like he was falling asleep. I reached up to his shoulder and asked if he was okay, and he suddenly turned toward me with a green face and his deep, raspy voice saying, "I didn't know I was coming here to DIE! The exhaust fumes are coming through the floor and I can't breathe any more. I'm gonna DIE! Let's get out of here!" Well, I absolutely lost it! I laughed so hard that I couldn't breathe. He just looked so funny with a green face. We asked the driver to take us back to the house and Georgie had to go lie down for a few hours. He told me to find a new driver, because he was not getting in that car again. Fortunately, we had a Gladney driver for the rest of the trip.

I was happy to have the same driver, Tafessa, that we had on our previous trip. He told us to keep the windows up for safety reasons. There are so many people begging in the streets and they can be dangerous. The only problem was that it was so hot, and there was no air conditioning in the car. So Georgie rolled down his window anyway, and said he would be on the lookout and ready to handle any trouble. There we were at a red light and a man came up to the car, begging. Georgie shook his head no and tried to ignore him. Then suddenly, the guy stuck his hand right into the window and in Georgie's face, to show he had six fingers on one hand. Georgie yelled and shoved the guy's hand back out, rolling up the window. Then he snapped his head around so fast toward me, and with his deep, raspy voice saying, "HEY, 'I'" (my family nickname), "DID YOU SEE DAT? HE HAD SIX FINGAS!" I thought he was going to get whiplash from snapping his head so hard. I literally lost it again! I was laughing so hard that I had tears streaming down my face! I told him *I* was going to die this time, because I couldn't breathe from laughing so hard. Even Solomon and Tafessa were hysterical. Needless to say, he didn't open his window anymore.

We were busy every day. We visited the Gladney office and foster homes to see the children. Ryan and Abby were no longer there, but Anbez, Travis, and Joanna had taken their place. It was a joy to see Belay too. They said they considered me a part of their team, because they had heard our name so many times since we left. Because of our blog and speaking ministry, many adoptive families that had since come through the agency mentioned our name as being instrumental in influencing their adoption journey. When we visited the baby houses, Solomon was shocked to see so many babies at once. He had never held one, and had no idea there were so many children who were orphaned and waiting to be adopted. We were able to hold the two babies of our friends, the Georges, that were soon going home to America. Today they live just a few miles from our home.

Gladney also set up another meeting with our precious birth mother. Solomon was able to meet her and served as our translator, because she does not speak English. She was shocked and so happy to see me back in Ethiopia so soon. We visited for several hours, hugged and cried, took video and were so glad to see each other again. I brought her lots of photos and art work the children had made for her. We had another divinely appointed visit.

Ever since Solomon had arrived at the orphanage, he ate injera with soup broth for three meals every day. Sometimes they would get dry pasta with nothing on it. It was such a blessing to introduce him to so many new foods and experience many "firsts" with him as his new mama. We took him for ice cream and I bought every flavor, since he had never had it before. I lined them along the table and told him to taste them all and tell me his favorite. When he chose strawberry, I called him Papa's boy, because that is Jerry's favorite too! Unfortunately, he got a brain freeze and headache because he had never eaten anything that cold before. His favorite foods were pancakes and eggs, pasta with tomato sauce, steak, and pizza.

Solomon had never told the boys at Kolfe that I was coming, because he said he wanted to surprise them. I think he also wasn't sure if I was really going to show up. It was so surreal to be on the road back to Kolfe. I honestly never thought I would be back so soon. This time the ride there was filled with excitement and joy, wanting to see all those beautiful smiles again. When I got out of the car, the boys recognized me right away and started to shout, "MAMA EILEEN!" They came running and asked for kisses and hugs. They started telling me their memories of our Mama Hug party, and mimicked me by lining up and kissing each other and laughing. They told me that no one had ever done that before or since. Many people had been coming to visit just like I said they would, and then one boy shouted, "But none of them hug and kiss us like you, Mama Eileen." With that, I responded, "Do you want another one?" And a bunch of them yelled yes, and all came running toward me with their arms wide open. So there I stood a second time, hugging and kissing all these precious boys, telling them God loved them and had miraculously brought me back to give them another Mama's hug. Many of them talked with me for a long time and said they often reminisced about my last visit. They even had contests among them to see who got the most hugs.

This time, Georgie was there taking video. The boys knew from Ryan that we were instrumental in all the renovations that had taken place and were thanking me for everything. They were excited to point out all the new changes. I was especially happy to see Tesfa again, the young man who had told me their government had no money, no one ever helped them, and everyone, including God, had forgotten about them. He gave me a big hug and smile and said, "You kept your word. Thank you for everything you have done for us. May God bless you." I reminded him that it was God who loved them and not only brought me there twice now, but also brought many other people to show them they are loved and not forgotten. I was on the tour of the compound once again and in awe of how much had been improved. They all had new mattresses and blankets and new windows with curtains on them. The buildings were freshly painted inside and out, the kitchen was remodeled, and they even had new pots and dishes. The grounds were beautifully leveled and landscaped, with no more ankle-breaking safety hazards. Even their soccer field and goal posts were redone. It was amazing!! It was not the same place I had left two years earlier. Gladney was faithful to minister to the Kolfe Orphanage, and my heart was overflowing with joy. I honestly could not believe the difference from my last visit.

For the next two weeks, we spent a lot of time with the boys. We brought a car load of fruit and a new TV, and just talked with them for hours. It was such a joy to fellowship with them again. They also had a lot of questions after watching the *Jesus* film that Georgie played for them. I was able to teach them about the Scriptures and the Lord Jesus Christ. Two of the young men asked me to help them pray to receive Jesus as their Savior. Solomon also shared that as a result of our relationship, and reading the Bible for the last two years, he had asked Jesus to be his Savior, and had come to know God in a whole new way. It was an amazing opportunity!

While we were there, we witnessed the transfer of twenty-seven boys who had aged out of the younger children's orphanage, Kebebe Tsehai, to Kolfe. We watched them walking around, crying and being so scared. We were heartbroken and wanted to do something to cheer them up. So we went shopping at the Mercato market and bought them all a new backpack with soccer team emblems, and filled with school supplies and goodies. They were so excited and smiled when we presented them all with their gifts. I also did a lot of hugging and kissing on them. I took the older boys aside and asked them to remember when they had first arrived at Kolfe, and asked them to help these little guys feel welcomed. I asked them to treat them the way they would want to be treated, and many of them happily went to the little guys and started talking and playing around with them. I also asked them to be good role models for the boys, because that is what God wanted them to do.

Georgie met two young brothers, and for some reason said they immediately took a special place in his heart. He spent a lot of time with them and told me he fell in love with them. He took them on a shopping spree for new clothes, shoes, and a hearty lunch. He kept saying he didn't know why, but these boys were very special to him, and he wished he could adopt them. Knowing that wasn't possible, he told me, "Hey, 'I,' when we get home you have to work especially hard to get my boys adopted, so that I can visit them in the USA." As it turned out, we were instrumental in getting them adopted and they now live in Oregon!

18 Solomon's Graduation

If any of you lacks wisdom, he should ask God, who gives generously to all without finding fault, and it will be given to him. But when he asks, he must believe and not doubt, because he who doubts is like a wave of the sea, blown and tossed by the wind (James 1:5-6).

I wanted to do something special for Solomon's graduation, like we did with our other children. I knew I wouldn't be back to visit him for a long time and wanted to make a special memory with him. He had never been outside of the orphanage, so we arranged for a two-day retreat to visit the Kuriftu Resort. It is known as a place for the rich and famous and is absolutely beautiful. Even the two-hour drive out into the countryside was refreshing. We invited our driver, Tafessa, and my friend Misganaw to join us, and the five of us had a wonderful time. We ate at the fine dining restaurant overlooking the lake, were pampered with a spa massage, and devoured the aroma and view of the tropical flowering scenic landscape and warm sunshine glistening on the lake. The entire resort was just breathtaking. We talked and laughed for hours, enjoying the outdoor fireplace into the wee hours under the moonlight. It was relaxing and refreshing for us all. Before we knew it, it was time to head back to Addis for the graduation ceremony.

We bought Solomon a suit and new shoes for the ceremony and he looked so handsome. It was his first time to get dressed up. He had told me that people always knew the orphans, because they were the students who wore tattered clothes at graduations. Gladney has since added a new ministry to provide dress clothes for the orphans at graduation through humanitarian aid donations. Solomon had also told me that if I couldn't come to his graduation, he was not going to attend either. He was the only orphan in this school of 400 students, and he didn't want to be there all alone when all the other students had a family. Nothing like feeling a little pressure! I was so grateful the Lord made a way when it all seemed so impossible.

The ceremony was at the Convention Center in downtown Addis Ababa. It was a huge event, similar to a typical high school graduation ceremony here in the USA. There were over 1,000 people there and we were the only Caucasians. When we arrived, Solomon was sitting with his class and asked me to show him where our seats were. He said he wanted to see me when he was on the stage receiving his diploma. I assured him he would find me, because I was the only white lady with red hair in the whole place. He was so excited to introduce me to all of his classmates, holding my hand the whole time. Several of them said, "He always talked about having a mom in the USA, but we didn't believe him." All the people were surprised to see us white folks there.

Misganaw joined us too, and was able to translate the ceremony for us because everything was spoken in Amharic. This is one of the most ancient languages spoken today and it is unique to Ethiopia. Ethiopian culture moves at a very slow pace compared to the USA. The ceremony started two hours late, and then it lasted for three more hours. Misganaw said this was normal.

We listened as they finally called each student to the stage, and watched as they grabbed their diploma, shook the hand of the school director and a few faculty members, and went cheering off the stage. There was a lot of clapping, cheering, and family support for each student. Every once in a while, I heard a very unique chant, and Misganaw said it was for the honor students. When it was announced that a particular student had a high score, they would let out this strange sounding chant that I had never heard before. Finally, they called Solomon's name. We stood up, cheering and clapping, with Georgie taking video. We were so proud of him. All eyes were on the two white people standing up and screaming. Then I watched Solomon walk up the stairs and slowly shake the hand of every single person on the stage. He started with the person at the bottom of the stairs and went to everyone, even the people unpacking the boxes of diplomas. He got to the director and received his diploma, and then turned to look right at me. He held his diploma out toward me and blew me a kiss, saying, "Thank you, Mama!" Needless to say, I was a bucket of tears and using lots of tissues!

I noticed Solomon was the only student out of the 400 who shook the hand of every person on the stage from top to bottom. He demonstrated his gratitude for the privilege of getting an education, and wanted to show his appreciation to everyone involved in the graduation ceremony. I was overflowing with joy and thanking God for the miracle and privilege of allowing me to be there to witness this miraculous day, and to be involved in Solomon's life. When he blew me that kiss, I just lost it. I started to think of what that day would have been like had I not been there. Would he have missed it? I was standing in awe!

After the diplomas were distributed, it was time to announce the valedictorian. It was taking a long time and then suddenly Misganaw said, "Wouldn't it be amazing if Solomon was the valedictorian?" I looked at him with confidence, saying that would take a miracle because he had failed the national exam two years earlier and had been kicked out of school. I was also sure Solomon would have told me if he was. Then Misganaw responded, "Wait a minute! When Solomon was called for his diploma they announced that he had a very high score. That was only mentioned for him and one other female student. The other students were announced with a 'high score,' not 'very high'." Then Georgie said, "Are you kidding me? Let me tell you guys right now, if they announce he is the valedictorian, I am going to fall out right here." I seconded that motion. My heart started to race as I began to ponder that dream for Solomon. We started to fantasize about what a miracle that would be, but we honestly thought it was impossible.

There we were, literally sitting on the edge of our seats, looking wide-eyed at the stage. The director spoke in Amharic, I am assuming giving details about the student, and then he called, "SOLOMON BEKELE!" We looked at each other in shock, with mouths wide open, and started to scream, clap, and jump up and down. I could see Solomon from where I was sitting and he didn't get up. He was just sitting there. The crowd was cheering and clapping, but no one was getting up toward the stage. We quickly sat down, thinking we had heard the man wrong, and just kept staring at Solomon. It seemed like an eternity as we sat there looking around for the valedictorian to stand up. Then they called his name a second time, but again he didn't get up. Everyone was still clapping and cheering, but no one was standing up from the class. We were just sitting there looking at each other, wondering what was happening. Then all of a sudden, Solomon stood up and started to walk toward the stage, shaking his head in disbelief. The crowd was now in a loud roar, chanting and howling and clapping, and giving him a standing ovation. Now I was not only the only red-headed white lady in this crowd of 1,000 people, but I was the only 'jumping up and down, clapping, crying, and screaming "THAT'S MY SON!!" white lady' in the crowd. Georgie and Misganaw were jumping, screaming, and crying right there with me, and we must have been a real sight to see. We were hugging and kissing each other and screaming at the top of our lungs! Georgie had the video camera rolling, but it turned out to be not a pretty sight to watch. That camera was swinging all over the place as he fell out like he had predicted. We were quite the spectacle in more ways than one.

Solomon finally got to the stage and again was shaking hands with everyone. Then he was presented with a huge three-foot high trophy and a medal around his neck. He walked to the front of the stage, held it up in the air, looked at me, and blew me another kiss. Again he mouthed the words "Thank you, Mom, I love you!" and I just lost it again! I was shaking the hardest I ever had. My knees wanted to give out from under me. I felt like I was in a dream and everything was spinning. It was absolutely surreal and unbelievable!

We gathered our belongings and headed for the stage, so I could get my hands on my boy. The crowd had gathered in front of us and we were pushing and announcing we were coming through. When I finally got to Solomon, he grabbed me and started to cry. He was shaking too! I cupped my hands on his face and just kissed him all over it. Then I looked him right in the eyes, saying, "Solomon, why didn't you tell me you were the valedictorian, and why didn't you stand up when they called your name?" In tears he said, "Mama, I didn't know. I thought maybe they called the wrong name or maybe there was another student with the same name as mine. This is a miracle, Mama, I didn't know!"

Then I said, "Solomon if you are so smart, why did you fail the national exam two years ago?" To which he responded, "Mama, until God brought you into my life I never had HOPE! I never studied and I thought I had no future. No one cared about me. Not even God. But when God brought you and Papa into my life and you paid for my school, I wanted to make you proud. I studied so hard and I prayed for God to help me with every exam. This is a miracle from God, Mama!"

We stood there in shock, sobbing in each other's arms. There was a huge crowd forming a line to congratulate him, so I let go of him and stepped aside. I had to hold tissues on my face, catching the tears that were pouring out of my eyes. I watched him beaming with joy, as hundreds of people congratulated him. He was basking in his finest moment.

I stood in the corner and began to reminisce back to the first day I had seen him at the orphanage. His head hung low as he was kicking rocks, looking like he had the weight of the world on his shoulders. I had never seen such sadness and hopelessness in someone's face. That was only two years before, and now he stood beaming with joy and a sense of pride and confidence that was radiant. Then another flood of thoughts went racing through my mind. What if I'd had my way and we had never gone to visit Kolfe? I was praying for God to thwart Ryan's plans that day! What if I hadn't handed the boys that piece of paper with my e-mail address? What if Solomon had never sent me that e-mail? What if I hadn't prioritized his e-mails, even though my life was so hectic? What if he hadn't gotten the scholarship and we hadn't sent the money to keep him in the school? Would he have been one of the homeless boys begging in the streets? What if I hadn't come to his graduation? Would he have come alone or not at all? Would he have missed this? What if I had ignored all those whispers from the Lord? What if I was just too busy or thought it was just too crazy to obey? Look at all the MIRACLES we would have missed!

After the graduation ceremony, the director of the school personally invited us to attend a special traditional luncheon back at the school campus. Misganaw's family also had planned a special graduation party at their house for Solomon to invite his friends.

Misganaw's dad joined us at the Convention Center and couldn't believe Solomon's good news. He hugged me, saying, "Thank you for everything you have done for this boy. He is very lucky to have you." Then he said, "I know you don't speak Amharic and you don't realize that everyone in the crowd is talking about you. They are all saying that you are an amazing woman to come all the way from America to take care of this orphan boy. They say he is very lucky to have you and they are proud of him for being the valedictorian. They are saying it is because of you that he had this opportunity. You are famous here too, not just Solomon." As I listened to him, my mind raced back to the night I had picked up Ellie from her Guatemala trip, just a few months earlier. This was exactly like the testimony Ellie had shared about the director of the orphanage there, who was now becoming a pastor. I just stood there, praising the Lord for His goodness.

We found out that Solomon had graduated with a 98.7 GPA and that he hadn't even taken the final exam. He was in the hospital with food poisoning and they would not let him take a makeup exam.

When we got back to the school campus, we couldn't wait another minute to call Jerry. It was 4:00 a.m. USA time, but we just had to tell him the good news. He too was in shock, thinking he was dreaming. We celebrated at both parties and had a wonderful time. Solomon never wiped the smile off of his face the rest of the day. Misganaw's family had a big cake in his honor, and he told me this was the first time he had ever had a cake with his name on it. They had the house decorated with Ethiopian grass on the floor, banners on the walls, and lots of traditional food, soda, and fruit. Then Misganaw's mom put on a traditional coffee ceremony in Solomon's honor as well. When the other Kolfe boys arrived at Misganaw's house, they did not believe Solomon was the valedictorian. They all said he was the worst student of them all. After all, he had failed the national exam and was about to be out of the orphanage. How could this be? No one could believe the transformation taking place in his life. Everyone was so happy for him. In the middle of the party, my cell phone rang, and it was Belay inviting us to join him with ten American couples that night for a traditional Ethiopian dinner and dance ceremony at the Fasika Restaurant. When I told him about Solomon, he said, "That is amazing. This is even more reason to celebrate; bring him along."

So after the five-hour graduation ceremony and two parties, we headed out for a night on the town. When we arrived, several of the American families recognized us from our blog and were so excited to meet Solomon in person. He was like a celebrity to them and when I made an announcement to the group about his valedictorian status, they all applauded and gave him a standing ovation. During the evening, one couple gave him a handwritten note with $45 in it. They told him they were so proud of him.

The entertainment of customary Ethiopian music and dancing began. It is very unique to Ethiopia and nothing like I have ever seen. Solomon had never seen it either. At the end of the dancers' performance, they walked into the audience and invited people to dance with them. All of a sudden, one of the male dancers came right to me and asked me to dance. I had never heard this kind of music or seen this style of dancing, but I love to dance and was willing to give it a try. He was trying to teach me how to do some of the traditional moves, which are kind of like moving your neck back and forth like a turkey, but at the speed of lightning. I tried a few times and then decided it was more fun to dance my way, so I let loose. I started to break out in some disco moves, waving my arms and having a great old time, grooving to the beat of the music. This guy stood back, his eyes and mouth opened wide, and he started to mimic my moves instead. He was looking into the crowd, laughing, when suddenly the entire restaurant started cheering and clapping for us. They broke into hysterics as they turned on their video cameras.

Everyone was clapping and laughing so hard, and Belay and his sister had tears streaming down their cheeks. When I looked over at Solomon, he was in shock with his eyes and mouth wide open too. I think I was embarrassing him, just like a mom is supposed to do to her kids, right? He had his camera going while he was laughing and I could tell he was blushing. Georgie had his video going and was also laughing the whole time. It was so much fun. When we were leaving the restaurant, the group of ten Gladney drivers all came to me, laughing so hard, saying they had all watched my performance and had never seen an American adoptive mom break out like that before. For the next few days, I was the talk of the town, and one of the drivers even presented me with a CD of Ethiopian music to take home.

The time flew by so quickly and the day came when I had to say goodbye to Solomon. Solomon cried so hard there was literally a puddle on the floor of the car. The driver even stopped the car, ran into a store and bought a box of tissues for him. Everyone kept trying to comfort him and spoke in Amharic a lot. He was inconsolable and we all felt terrible. He kept apologizing and saying he just couldn't help it. I was literally holding him in my arms all day. He couldn't eat and just kept his head down, crying. He told me the tears were coming from his heart and not his eyes. We both didn't know when, or even if, we would see each other again. I had no idea what was going to happen next. When I would think about it, I just saw a blank screen with no vision on the horizon.

I was happy that Solomon had a good education now, but because he was no longer a student and turning nineteen years old, the government was going to kick him out of the orphanage. He had not one living relative and was all alone in Ethiopia. I was so heavy-hearted, and knew I needed to help him find a job and a place to live. The problem was that the streets of Addis Ababa were full of people with college degrees begging for food. The housing was expensive and I didn't know what to do. I was asking Gladney and Cherokee and all my contacts to help me, but there was nothing on the horizon. Misganaw's family had agreed to let him stay with them temporarily, until I could figure something else out. But what was it going to be?

I hugged and kissed him goodbye at the airport and walked into the terminal, feeling the weight of his life and future on my shoulders. I cried and prayed all the way home. "Lord, what now? Please show me how to help Solomon from here!"

Georgie took fourteen hours of video, tons of photos, and we came home with a new story to tell. God taught us the importance and the impact one can have just by getting involved in the life of an orphan. Just by writing letters and being a support from across the world, we can give them hope for a future and show them that God cares for them. I had no idea just what an impact my e-mails and my time and attention were having on Solomon's life.

We can't change the world of orphans, but we can change an orphan's world, one at a time. Orphans need to know God and His

Holy Word. They need to know someone in the world knows their name and cares about them. They need an education and clothes and someone to cheer them on and love them. They need HOPE!

I am asking everyone who hears this story to get involved in the life of an orphan. You can pray for them, sponsor them, or adopt them. You can visit them on a mission trip and become a pen pal like we did. You can support their orphanage. You can get involved with the Christian Alliance for Orphans and network with numerous ministries working with orphans. You can donate to Show Hope, who gives grants to adoptive families, and works with special needs orphans in China. God says pure and undefiled religion is to care for orphans and widows in their distress. Not everyone is called to adopt, but everyone can do something! Please don't miss your opportunity to be the hands and feet of Jesus that can make a difference in the life of an orphan.

19 What Now, Lord?

Hear my cry, O God; attend unto my prayer. From the end of the earth will I cry unto thee, when my heart is overwhelmed; lead me to the rock that is higher than I. For thou has been a shelter for me, and a strong tower from the enemy (Psalm 61:1-2 KJV).

Even though I was so busy at home, my heart and mind wandered to Ethiopia daily as I prayed for Solomon. I was praying for the Lord to show me how to help him with his future and I was expecting instructions. While in Ethiopia I was able to get him a cell phone, and a friend donated a laptop and air card for Internet service. We were able to Skype with Jerry while I was there, and the kids got to see Solomon, which made them all so happy. We knew he was going to leave the orphanage soon and needed to insure we had a means of communication to reach him in a moment's notice.

Shortly after I arrived home, Solomon and I started the Kolfe Mama Ministry, for the purpose of duplicating what the Lord did with us to bless more boys. They were watching Solomon's life turn around since we started our relationship, and we both wanted them to have the same blessings. We matched several boys with families, encouraging them to become pen pals. I suggested they send a Bible to teach the boys about the Scriptures, with the hope they would come to know the Lord Jesus. We also encouraged support of their education, but specifically not to send money or material gifts. I was concerned the boys would be polluted by materialism, as well as be in jeopardy if word got out they had money. As long as Solomon was there, they were using his computer to correspond and he was translating for them. Several of the boys started to use the Internet café as well.

I was very concerned about giving strangers access to the boys; but was comfortable with families that had already been approved for adoption, because they were cleared through CIS and FBI security background checks. The other priority for me was that these families desired to teach the boys the gospel. After we matched about fifteen boys, we had peace that it was time to stop.

Several of the families actually got to visit the boys in Ethiopia and some of the boys were even adopted. This confirmed again that the Lord indeed had planned for more than my just attending Solomon's graduation on that trip.

It was the beginning of November 2009 and I had a dream. We were speaking at a conference of 500 people. I was standing on the stage, ready to share the story about Solomon. I was pointing to the screen where we usually show a video. A light was shining on it, but instead of the video playing, Solomon walked out from behind the curtain with his Bible in his hand and he put it on the podium. Everyone gasped and then started to applaud with a standing ovation. We were all shocked to see him in person. He stood at the podium and started to share his testimony.

This dream was so real that I jumped up in my bed and my heart was racing. Jerry woke up and asked what was wrong. I told him my dream and that I thought God was going to bring Solomon here to the United States to be a part of our speaking ministry. I shared this dream with everyone at breakfast and then I even told Solomon about it. I had never had a dream about him like that before.

Solomon told me he wanted to study computers and possibly own an Internet café in Ethiopia. I started praying about finding another school in Ethiopia for him. I was also sending e-mails to my contacts there for possible job opportunities. I was asking the Lord what the purpose was in Him bringing Solomon into our lives, when we seemed to be unable to really help him from so far away. Then I realized if we were only in his life to pray for him and be a sounding board; that was enough.

Go to Southeastern College

Just a few weeks later, I was driving home with my three little boys. It was late afternoon, rainy and cold, and I was trying to beat the evening rush hour traffic. Ellie called to ask how much longer before I would be home, because the twinettes were about to wake up from their nap and she really needed to finish her chemistry homework. So now the pressure was on. I was also thinking about what to make for dinner. Then all of a sudden I heard the whisper, *"Go to Southeastern College and ask for a scholarship for Solomon."* I literally looked up into the sky through my windshield and said, "What? They don't teach computers there. Solomon wants to study computers." I shook it off and just kept driving. Then I heard it again, *"Go right now to Southeastern College."*

The Southeastern Baptist Theological Seminary and Southeastern College are on the same campus right in the heart of our town, Wake Forest. We live within walking distance of this school. My daughter Melissa graduated from and met her husband there. Jonathan and Ellie have both taken classes there as well. It is a school that sends out missionaries and pastors, but they do not have any computer technology degree programs. So I was confused about this option for Solomon. But the closer I got to home, the more I knew I must obey.

I called Ellie and said, "Honey, I know I told you I was coming home, but God just told me I have to go to SEBTS right now and ask for a scholarship for Solomon. I am going to stop in the driveway and I need you to run out a copy of the *Wake Weekly* newspaper with the story of our family in it. I will try to hurry back home."

Ellie responded, "You're kidding? Okay, Mom, I guess you better go. I will get the paper and meet you in the driveway, but please hurry."

The boys were not happy either. They wanted to stay at home with Ellie, but she was working on homework, so they had to go with me. Do you know how three little boys, ages five and six, can whine? They wanted to go home and eat. I explained that we had to go on an assignment from the Lord regarding their brother Solomon. This was the most stressful time of the day and really not convenient. But I knew I must obey.

I was now on a mission, with my adrenaline pumping. It is difficult to explain when you hear the voice of God telling you to do something. We walked into the admissions office and I asked to speak to someone in charge of international students. I was directed to a young man, Matthew, who was talking with someone at his desk. He turned to me and asked if he could help me, like it was going to be short and sweet.

I told him I needed to speak to someone about a scholarship for an orphan boy from Ethiopia. He very matter-of-factly looked at me and said, "We don't give scholarships for international students. They have to pay for it, and if you are interested, I will give you an information packet." He started to reach in his desk for the packet when I said, "I know this sounds crazy, but God just told me to come here and ask for a scholarship, so I need to speak to someone about it." He just glared at me for a moment and then repeated that there was no scholarship program available for international students.

I stood with three little boys who wanted to leave very badly, and now I had to convince this guy that I was not crazy. I began to tell him I was involved in orphan care ministry, and I asked if he was aware that the Southern Baptist Convention had just passed a resolution in June 2009, stating that it is the responsibility of the church to care for orphans. This is a Southern Baptist Theological Seminary and Christian College and God told me to come here. So I cannot leave until I speak with someone about it.

At this point, poor Matthew was getting very frustrated with me. When he realized I was not going to give up, he told me to go to the finance department and ask someone there, but he was sure I would get the same answer. I think he was aggravated that I was not walking out the door already. I then asked for the application packet and he reluctantly handed me one. As I started out the door, I turned around to speak to him. I walked back toward him and extended my hand to shake hands and said, "What was your name again?"

"Matt," he responded. I then added, "Matt, I just want you to know that I believe with all my heart you are going to see me again. Remember, my name is Eileen Mestas and you are going to meet my son Solomon from Ethiopia. So don't forget this day!"

As I walked out of the door, I knew this guy thought I was an absolute lunatic. So off to the finance department we marched in the cold, dreary weather. Of course it had to be on the other side of the campus. It was now getting close to the end of the day, about 4:30, and I walked in and greeted the young man at the desk. I told him I was looking for information regarding a scholarship for an international student and he gave me the same answer. "We don't have scholarships for international students. We only give partial scholarships for domestic students, and they are not anywhere near the cost for international student expenses." So I repeated again, "I know this is crazy, but God told me to come here to inquire about a scholarship for an international student, an orphan boy from Ethiopia. I can't leave here until I speak to someone about this! There has to be someone I can talk to."

To which he responded, "The only person who would be able to talk about that would be the President, Dr. Akin, I guess. But I think he is gone for Thanksgiving, so you can ask for his assistant, Debbie." I answered, "Okay, then, where is his office?"

"Well, you have to walk across the campus to Stealey Hall," he replied. "Thank you very much for your help," I answered. I took the boys by the hand and we darted out the door, running back to the building we had originally started in ... of course! It was now getting closer to 5:00, and I knew everyone was going to be leaving soon.

We walked into Dr. Akin's office and I asked the receptionist if I could speak to Debbie. She was standing there talking to someone and turned to me and said, "Hi, I'm Debbie, how can I help you?"

"Hi, may I speak to you for a few minutes, please?"

"Sure, come right here into my office." We walked into her office and I proceeded to sit the three boys in the chairs at her desk. I bent down and looked right into their faces, explaining that it was imperative they be quiet. "Don't get out of the chair, just be quiet and let me speak to this nice lady without interruptions. We are almost finished and we will go home to eat dinner after this discussion."

I then took a deep breath and sighed, as I turned to Debbie, who was now sitting at her desk. I took the newspaper article out of my purse and laid it right in front of her explaining, "This is a story about our family that explains all about our adoption and orphan care ministry. You can read this later, but I just wanted to show you that I am here with a legitimate ministry and reason.

"I know this sounds crazy, but I was driving home from Raleigh trying to beat rush hour traffic and thinking about dinner tonight, when I believe the LORD told me to come here and ask for a scholarship for a young man living in an orphanage in Ethiopia.

He just graduated as valedictorian of a school of 400 students and he was the only orphan in the school."

She sat there with her eyes fixed on mine. I asked, "Are you familiar with the resolution that the Southern Baptist Convention passed in June 2009 that says it is the church's responsibility to care for orphans?"

To my surprise she said, "Yes, I read it myself."

"Oh, thank the Lord," I replied. I immediately felt like now she would understand and have ears to hear me. I felt like the Holy Spirit was speaking through me as I said, "I believe the Lord sent me here on behalf of a young orphan boy in Ethiopia named Solomon. He is a bright student and the Lord wants you to give him a scholarship to come here. The Southern Baptist Convention's resolution stated that we are to be engaged in orphan care. This is the Southeastern Baptist Theological Seminary and Christian College. We live a few blocks from here and Solomon can live with us, so you won't have to give him room and board. All you really have to do is put another chair in an existing classroom, and that really isn't going to cost you anything."

She suddenly looked at me and then took her glasses off, laid them on her desk, and began to cry. I stood there so surprised, and realized immediately that her heart was touched and she heard me. I too began to cry. She said, "I believe you are a divine appointment standing at my desk. Dr. Akin is out of town this week for the Thanksgiving holiday, but give me all of your information and I personally will speak to him about this." I was now shaking all over, crying tears of joy and thanking her from the bottom of my heart. She told me she would show him the newspaper article and that she would get back to me as soon as he made a decision. I joyfully took the boys by the hand and headed home for dinner.

I opened the door to leave, and I could see a vision of Solomon walking across the campus wearing his backpack. I immediately lost it and told the boys we needed to pray for this to come true. We walked across the grass to a gazebo garden area where the boys and I sat for the next twenty minutes. I told them that the LORD hears and answers the prayers of His children and asked them to please pray that HE would give us the miracle of Solomon coming to attend this school.

I was crying and could not talk. I asked them to pray to the Lord for this miracle. I told them to remember this day, because I felt in my heart that this was a very special day in our faith journey. God was going to use their specific prayers in Solomon's life. I believed we were going to see Solomon walking across this campus. We sat there for the next twenty minutes, and I listened to our sweet six-year-olds, Jeremiah and James, and five-year-old Josiah, pleading with God to bring their big brother Solomon here to go to this school that will teach him about God. We were sitting on holy ground and this was indeed a special day.

When we finally got home, Grandma had prepared dinner, since I was running so late. What a blessing to have her in my life. The kids were happy and I was exhausted and just wanted to go to sleep. It was another momentous day.

20 A Scholarship for Solomon

"I tell you the truth, if you have faith as small as a mustard seed, you can say to this mountain, 'Move from here to there' and it will move. Nothing will be impossible for you" (Matthew 17:20-21).

It was late Friday afternoon two weeks later, and we still had not heard from Debbie at SEBTS. I was scheduled for a telephone interview with *Focus on the Family*, Monday at 2:30 p.m. and was hoping to share testimony Solomon had been awarded a scholarship. I was afraid to be a nuisance, but I wanted to see if there was any news yet. So at 4:30 p.m., I decided to call.

Debbie actually answered her telephone and I said, "Hello, Debbie, I am sorry to bother you. I just wanted to know if you have heard anything about the scholarship for Solomon. We have an interview with *FOF* on Monday and I was hoping to share this story with them."

She responded, "Your ears must be ringing ... I am sitting right here with Dr. Akin and he has the newspaper story about your family in his hands. He just said that if you can get Solomon here from Ethiopia, he will award him a full tuition scholarship!" I burst into tears and yelled into the room where the whole family was waiting with wide eyes and beating hearts. "He said YES!!! Solomon is getting a tuition scholarship to come to SEBTS!" We all started to scream and shout for joy, as we were overwhelmed with gratitude. She said Matthew, from the international student department, would call me on Monday to start the process. Needless to say, we all were crying and again in awe of what the Lord was doing. We continue to SEE HIM perform one miracle after another.

As we were rejoicing in awe, I realized Solomon didn't know anything about this yet. I hadn't told him anything, because I wasn't sure if it was ever going to happen. But now it was time to call him with this great news. It was the middle of the night in Ethiopia and we woke him up. "Solomon, this is Mama, I need to talk to you about something very important. How would you like to come to the United States to study in a Christian school?"

He responded in a groggy voice, "What, Mama?"

I proceeded to tell him this testimony: "I know you told me you want to study computers, but Solomon, I think God may have other plans for you. He has given you the gift of a full tuition scholarship at the same college Melissa and Randy graduated from. But they don't have a computer program. The College at Southeastern is a part of the Southern Baptist Theological Seminary that trains people to make disciples to go into the world to fulfill the Great Commission. The focus is to equip people to teach the gospel. It is very important that you go talk to God and ask Him if this is really what He wants for you. This school is going to be very academically challenging. It has the reputation of having very high standards of excellence. You will have to work very hard and understand that if this is God's plan for you, He will help you. I don't want you to make a decision right now. You need to pray to God. This is not from me; it was not my idea to do this. This is not a sure thing yet, because we still have to get approval from the United States Immigration Department, and it is going to take a lot more miracles to make this happen. I honestly believe God has just presented this opportunity for you, but only He knows for sure what is going to happen." I told him I would call him the next day and we hung up.

Solomon was in shock just like we were. I was hoping he would really understand that I had nothing to do with this, and that it was imperative for him to seek the Lord for this huge decision. It was really between him and the Lord. When I spoke to him the next day he said, "Mama, if God wants me to be a pastor or missionary for Him, then that is what I will do. I will work hard for Him. I don't have to work in computers. I want to do whatever He wants me to do. That is the most important thing."

I told him to get ready for an amazing adventure and to realize that God has a plan for his good, no matter how this pans out. I was afraid of getting his hopes up and him being devastated if he didn't get approved. Talk about adding more stress in my life! How much more could I handle?

By noon Monday, I had not heard anything from the international student department, so I decided to call Matthew myself. When he answered the telephone I said, "Hello, Matthew, I don't know if you remember me, but I was there two weeks ago asking for a scholarship for my Ethiopian orphan boy, Solomon. I heard from Dr. Akin's assistant, Debbie, that he has, in fact, awarded us a full tuition scholarship and I need to talk to you to get the process started."

There was an unusually long pause on the other end of the phone, and I wondered if I was disconnected. Then I heard a very serious and somber voice say, "Yes, I remember you. I was just sitting here right now preparing an e-mail to send you with some instructions."

I responded, "Well, instead of sending me an e-mail, can we discuss this right now?"

He hesitantly said, "Well, I guess so. I have a few questions I need to ask you. First of all, we are an educational institution and we are not here to bring orphans to the United States. All international students have to return to their country after they complete their studies. What kind of work does he want to do and which one of our degree programs is he interested in? What kind of ministry work is he involved in now?" He made me feel like he was annoyed that he had to deal with me again and that I was wasting his time.

I said, "Matthew, I would love to tell you about the ministry that Solomon is involved in, but it is going to take some time. Do you have time right now for me to tell you about this amazing young man?"

He somberly answered, "Yes, I guess we can talk now." So I began to tell him the amazing testimony of how I had met Solomon, about the blog, and Kolfe Mama Ministry. I told him how God had used our blog and speaking ministry to make Solomon famous in the church's awakening to the worldwide orphan crisis. I told him to 'Google' Solomon's name and see what came up, to verify my claims.

I ended with this statement, "Matthew, God has intentionally placed you in the middle of this miraculous journey. He has an amazing plan for Solomon, who two years ago was all alone in the orphanage, thinking he was forgotten by God and no one knew he existed. He had no hope for a future and was destined to be a homeless orphan with no education or skills. But GOD HAS ANOTHER PLAN! And we are called to help Him accomplish it. Matthew, as I told you two weeks ago, I believe with all my heart you are going to meet Solomon someday soon."

There was another long, silent pause and I thought he must have hung up a long time ago. Then suddenly I heard him say, "Wow, that was an amazing story. I understand better now and I am looking forward to meeting Solomon. Let me send you an e-mail with instructions on what you need to do next. I am looking forward to working with you and getting Solomon here." For a second I honestly thought someone else had gotten on the phone, because his attitude had changed and even his voice sounded different.

Dr. Akin gave Solomon a full tuition scholarship and waived all of the fees. However, the Federal Immigration Department requires that all students have at least $8,000 in a bank account to prove support for the first year. All international students are not allowed to work for the first year, which means they must prove they have support so as not to become destitute. They do not qualify for any type of aid from our government. We had to submit notarized documents that we would be financially responsible for him and an affidavit from the bank for the $8,000. We are also responsible to ensure he has medical insurance coverage at all times. We are responsible for his behavior, i.e. any crime that may be committed or financial penalties he may incur, etc. Solomon also had to pass the TOEFL English proficiency exam.

I told Matthew that we could meet all the requirements, except we did not have $8,000 to put in his name in a bank account. So it was time to go to the LORD in prayer. I told Matthew we needed another miracle and I would let him know as soon as the Lord delivered it. I didn't see the point in moving forward until then. So we had a family prayer meeting and knew it was time to wait for another miracle!

21 Orphan Sunday Presentation

A father to the fatherless, a defender of widows, is God in his holy dwelling. God sets the lonely in families, ... (Psalm 68:5-6).

November is National Adoption Awareness month in the United States. Having been involved with The Christian Alliance for Orphans ministry for several years, we were praying for the Lord to use us to start an orphan care ministry at our church. The Orphan Care Sunday project was started through the Alliance, and we asked permission to give a presentation to help our new church get involved in the awakening movement. Our pastor agreed to give us twelve minutes, in both services on Sunday morning.

Now I have to tell you that when he said we had only twelve minutes, I was very disappointed. Normally when I speak at conferences, it is impossible to say everything in the usual thirty minute allotment, so what was going to be done in only twelve minutes? I told Jerry it was impossible to get anything accomplished, saying, "I will barely start to talk and time will be up, so what is the point?"

He responded, "Well, if we only have twelve minutes, at least it is better than nothing. We have to make the best of it and leave it in the Lord's hands." I knew he was right, but I was still upset.

We showed a video presentation the Alliance produced and then I shared a brief testimony of our adoption, our relationship with Solomon, and ministry to the Kolfe Orphanage. I talked as fast as I could, but I took twenty minutes in the first hour, and eighteen minutes in the second. It was so hard to get it all in, but we just prayed the Lord would move in the hearts of the people to SEE HIM and HIS desire for the church to awaken to the orphan crisis. The pastor wasn't too mad at me, but did make a comment about it.

At the end of the service, we had a table set up with information from *FamilyLife Today®* on how to get involved in orphan care. We gave Jeremiah, James, and Josiah the responsibility of passing out prayer cards for orphans. We are always teaching our children that our family is called to be missionaries, and our ministry is to educate the church on getting involved in the command of James 1:27. They were so excited and took their jobs very seriously. It was such a blessing to see them running after people who thought they could just walk out of the church empty-handed. They were literally chasing people down and handing them the prayer cards saying, "Please help the orphans waiting for a family." I stood there watching this precious sight of three little boys who were once orphaned themselves, pleading on behalf of the ones still left behind. They were only four and six years old, and I saw people literally crying tears as they watched them with passion and ownership of their own ministry.

During the presentation, I was surprised to see many people engaged and crying. Many of them thanked us. We had no idea how much of an impact those eighteen and twenty minutes had. The next Sunday when we got to church there were so many people telling us they were moved by the presentation. We learned that many of the Sunday school classes had spent the hour talking about it. Several people asked the pastor for another longer presentation. Requests were coming in to personally meet with us, because people felt God leading them to pursue adoption. One man handed Jerry a piece of paper with his telephone number, asking to meet with us that Wednesday night.

This was the first time we met Chris and Tracey Rafferty. They are a young couple with two little girls. We sat at their kitchen table and listened to their amazing testimony. Tracey said when it was announced that we were doing an Orphan Sunday presentation, she honestly wanted to get up and leave. She had a lot to do that day and motioned to her husband, but he did not want to leave. So, she sat there with her arms folded, puffing her breath and tapping her feet, just waiting for us to finish. But God had another plan!

As she sat through the presentation, learning statistics about the orphan crisis, she began to cry. She was trying to fight the tears but couldn't, and neither could her husband. She knew right then that God was doing something. For the next several days, she could not stop crying and was arguing with God, because she did not want to adopt a child. But they both felt He was calling them into HIS plan.

Her husband came home from work one night and said the Lord told him they were to adopt a little boy from Bulgaria. She spent hours that week reading our blog and researching adoption. They realized together that the Lord did something in their hearts through our presentation, and this was why we were sitting at their kitchen table just a week later. We were all in tears.

I never dreamed such a short and rushed presentation could have such a powerful impact! We recommended the Gladney Adoption Agency because I knew for a fact that they adopt from Bulgaria. We highly recommend Gladney to everyone because we had such a wonderful experience with them. We have come to be great friends through all of the ministry the Lord has created for us to do.

Just when I thought we were wrapping up the evening, Tracey asked for the status of Solomon's scholarship process, since she had just read about it on our blog. We explained about the government requirement of $8,000 to be in his name in a bank account, and that we needed another miracle. The school could not issue the I-20 Visa to start the process until we had the money in the bank. As I was talking, they both were crying and looking at each other. We were crying most of the evening, so this was not unusual.

Then Chris suddenly said, "I don't know if you noticed, but Tracey has been kicking me under the table while you were talking. I know exactly what she is telling me. Eileen and Jerry, we want to give you a check for $8,000 right now before you leave." Jerry and I were absolutely shocked and I burst into tears. Jerry even said, "OH, NO, YOU CAN'T DO THAT!" They proceeded to explain that Tracey's father had passed away and left them some money. They believed there was no better way to use the money, and that her dad would be pleased to know it was being used to rescue orphans. I was shaking and in tears again! We had just met these people four hours ago, and they were giving us this money. We felt the presence of the Lord and knew this was a miracle for Solomon. So the next day, I called Matthew at SEBTS and told him this story. The Lord had given us the next miracle we prayed for.

When we were in Ethiopia the first time, the Lord laid on my heart that He was going to move us to a church where HE was going to raise up an orphan/adoption care ministry. Our previous church was made up of just a few families that we dearly loved, and they fully supported our adoption. But He was moving us out to be about HIS business. This was the first time in two years that we were presented with an opportunity to share our testimony in the church. As a result of that presentation, there was a buzz throughout the church of approximately 600 members, about adoption and orphan care. So the pastor decided to call a meeting to inquire about starting an official ministry at the church. When we walked into the first meeting, over 100 people showed up. I burst into tears and knew the Lord was indeed at work. Since then, they have officially launched an Adoption and Orphan Care Ministry at Open Door Baptist Church in Raleigh, North Carolina. They enrolled in the Abba Fund which helps finance adoptions with interest free loans for church members. They have a ministry to orphanages in Haiti and Mexico, and numerous families have started the adoption process, with several of them already being united as a family. And being the awesome God that He is, He also used that presentation to provide $8,000 for Solomon's next adventure.

Ellie spoke the truth when she said, "If God can create the world in seven days, surely He can do something at the church in twenty minutes." Another lesson learned about the faithfulness and power of God.

Please go to the Christian Alliance for Orphans website and get information about doing a presentation at your church. Seek the Lord's will for how He wants you to get involved with the awakening call for the church. I highly recommend attending the Summit Conference put on every year as well; you will not regret it!

http://www.christianalliancefororphans.org/

22 US Embassy Appointment

But if we hope for what we do not yet have, we wait for it patiently. In the same way, the Spirit helps us in our weakness (Romans 8:25-26).

The Lord gave Solomon a full tuition scholarship and provided the $8,000 in a bank account. Next was to pass the TOEFL English Proficiency exam. He registered to take the exam at the University of Addis Ababa, in Ethiopia. Once this was completed, the school here would issue an I-20 Visa and his packet would go to the United States Embassy for approval to be an international student. Students are permitted to stay in the United States as long as they are registered as a full-time student. Everyone told us the biggest hurdle in this process was to be approved by the US Embassy. The key requirement for all international students is to prove they will return to their country after graduation. They must prove residency, own real estate, have bank accounts, job security, and a family in their country. Orphans do not meet any of the requirements for international student status. They have no family, no permanent residence or real estate, no bank accounts or job security. We were told by many people on this journey not to get our hopes up, because the Embassy would be the end of the line.

Solomon took the TOEFL exam and said it was very difficult for him. He didn't think he passed, but we all knew it was in the Lord's hands. The results were going to be sent directly to SEBTS within two weeks. Three weeks later, Matthew called to tell me his results were in. "Solomon failed the exam!" My heart sank. But he said, "Dr. Akin saw the results and said that because Solomon had failed the national exam and then become valedictorian, he has proven a great work ethic. Living with your family here in America will make it easier for him to learn English. He is going to approve the I-20 Visa even though he did not pass the exam." Woohooo! Another miracle! He said the visa was going to be processed and would be ready for the Embassy in a few weeks. All we could do now was pray.

I was praying for wisdom on how we could convince the Embassy to approve his visa. The Lord was showing me that Solomon was already being used as a voice for the orphan through our ministry, as HE was creating the awakening in the church to care for orphans and widows. Then I remembered the dream I had about Solomon being on the stage with me in our ministry. We had just signed a contract to speak at the MidAtlantic Orphan Summit in Hershey, Pennsylvania in November 2010. I suddenly realized if Solomon's visa got approved, he would be here in time for that conference. So, I called my friend Dr. Brad Davidson, who was organizing the conference, and asked if he would give us another contract with Solomon's name on it, to prove that he was involved in the Orphan Care Ministry. Brad had traveled to Ethiopia the year before and had actually met Solomon. I told him about my dream and how I believed God was going to use Solomon at this conference. He agreed and sent me the contract to include in the visa request packet.

Then I contacted our pastor and asked for a letter stating he would be interested in working with Solomon in orphan care ministry when he returned to Ethiopia. The pastor gave me a letter to include in his packet too.

We are also very involved with Precept Ministry, Kay Arthur's ministry in Chattanooga, Tennessee, and Ellie loves to attend their summer boot camp program. We wanted Solomon to join her that summer and asked Kay for a scholarship for him. She agreed and sent us a letter awarding another scholarship to attend the camp. This was another proof that he was going to be studying the Word of God.

Solomon's visa request packet now had all of these documents, in addition to the I-20 Visa and SEBTS scholarship. The packet was sent to the US Embassy in Ethiopia via Fed Ex. Several days passed and they had not received it. So, Solomon went to the Fed Ex office in Addis Ababa to inquire. They found it sitting on someone's desk, which was not unusual in that country. He asked them to please deliver it to the Embassy, because he was waiting to make his appointment with them.

During this waiting zone, Jerry and I attended the Christian Alliance for Orphans Conference in Minneapolis. We were standing in a crowd of people talking, and someone asked about Solomon's status, because they read our blog. I shared a brief testimony of Solomon for the rest of the crowd and the current status that we were waiting for his appointment with the Embassy. Then I asked them all to pray because that was where the real battle was.

A man in the crowd, dressed in a very sharp-looking suit, handed me his business card and said, "If you have any problems with the Embassy, I may be able to help you. I work in Washington, DC." I took his card and started to cry as I said, "Okay, so this is obviously a divine appointment. If God brought us together today, I guess I am going to need you! I pray I won't, but thank you for offering and being available." I put his card right in my wallet and had a feeling I would be calling him soon.

We were able to share this testimony with many people at the CAFO conference. While having lunch with a group from Tennessee, we shared this story. When we finished, one of the people said, "This was the best break-out session I attended all weekend." His story has been inspiring many people to the plight of the orphan. There were people praying for Solomon all over the country.

Everything we read on the USCIS website said the decision would be determined right there at the embassy appointment. If they deny the visa, there is no appeal, and if they approve the visa, the student is permitted to travel no sooner than thirty days before matriculation.

Solomon's appointment was finally scheduled. We set our alarm to wake up in the middle of the night, the exact time he was meeting at the US Embassy in Addis. We prayed for the Lord to give him favor. We had prearranged to call him several hours after his appointment, and when we called he said, "They told me that if I don't hear from them within a month to come back." We were stunned and silent. What? Everything on the website said the decision was made at the appointment. This was not normal. We were grateful he wasn't denied, but couldn't understand what had happened. Then we realized he was an orphan that did not meet their requirements and that this was a very unique situation. They must be investigating the legitimacy of his packet. So we hung up the phone with Solomon, and I immediately ran to get the card of our contact in Washington, DC. I sent him an e-mail explaining the situation and he promptly responded, agreeing this was not a normal response.

He sent another e-mail with the contact information for our State Senator and Congressman, and told us to write them a letter asking for a status check on Solomon's visa request. I sent the letter right away. Without realizing it, Jerry also got this e-mail and he sent a request too. We don't always have time to talk to each other about things during the day and we didn't realize we were both doing the same thing.

The next day I got a call from Senator Kay Hagan's office. I explained the situation, and the man said he was going to personally call the US Embassy in Ethiopia for a status check. Jerry also got a call from a woman at the Embassy, and she said she was going to personally call the Ethiopia office as well. We were very impressed at the quick response from the Senator's office. We were in the waiting zone again.

One of the mandatory requirements to sponsor Solomon for his approval was to provide proof of income and his full financial support. As tradition would have it, every time we have been in an adoption process, Jerry lost his job. Right after we notarized all the documents and submitted Solomon's packet to the US Embassy, Jerry got laid off from his job again. The economy affected his sales territory in California, Nevada, and Arizona. The company decided to lay him off and hire someone who lived in the territory. So we were unemployed again! Until we began growing our family through adoption we were never out of work.

When I prayed and asked the Lord why this was happening, He simply said, *"There are a lot of people watching you. As I told you from the beginning, this is all about 'Me' getting the Glory and not you. Only I can make all things happen."* So, here we go again, on a journey of faith to prove we can't handle what the Lord has asked us to do. To God be the Glory!

23 Journey to the USA

... "We must obey God rather than men! We are witnesses of these things, and so is the Holy Spirit, whom God has given to those who obey him" (Acts 5:29, 32).

It was June 2010; I woke up as usual, with my feet hitting the floor and racing right to fifth gear. I was cleaning up breakfast, running the washing machine, dealing with two three-year-olds wanting me to play with them, the three boys who were playing with Legos, and I was praying to God for His anointing on this day. As I was starting to clean the downstairs bathroom, suddenly, it happened again.

I heard that whisper, *"Solomon is coming next Wednesday, so get everything ready."* I honestly stopped for a second and thought, *Oh, that was just my head telling me what my heart is aching for.* I felt a rush of adrenaline and started to get shaky. I went on to the next chore, trying to get things done, and I could not shake this thought in my head. My son Jonathan was standing at the kitchen sink and I finally had to say it out loud. "Jonathan, I think God just told me to get everything ready, because Solomon is coming next Wednesday." He turned his head toward me, smiled, and said, "Well, I guess you better get ready then, Mom, because you know what happens when God talks to you."

I kept asking myself if that was really God. We hadn't heard from the Embassy yet, so this didn't make sense! We were planning for our road trip to Tennessee for the Precept Bible Camp the following week. I knew if Solomon was going to make it, he had to be here no later than Friday, because we were leaving Saturday.

The Scriptures teach the Holy Spirit will guide and speak to us with wisdom and direction for our lives. So, when this happens to me, I want to be sure it is HIS leading. I humbly and cautiously step out in faith and obey what I am told to do. I always communicate with my family about what I think the LORD is leading and then I have to obey. Logically, it is crazy to hear a voice in your head. The fear of man says that I am going to look like an idiot or just plain crazy, if I tell anyone I hear God talking to me. But this is where FAITH steps in. If I ignore that little voice and don't do anything, how will I ever know if it really is GOD's voice? If I don't obey, then how will I be accomplishing God's will for my life? How will HE be able to use me for His purposes, if I don't listen and obey? If I do tell someone and then faithfully obey and it really comes true, then I know it was HIS voice and there are witnesses to prove it. The more this happens to me, the more familiar HIS voice becomes, and the more my faith grows. The Scriptures are full of testimony to people hearing God tell them what to do. The important factor is that everything must match up to the Holy Scriptures. God would never ask or lead us to do anything that is sinful. It is always about fulfilling HIS purpose to accomplish HIS will in the lives of HIS people.

After Jonathan agreed and encouraged me to get ready, I picked up the phone and called my friend Sabrina Freeland. We have been team teachers for the last two years in our Tapestry of Grace Homeschool Co-op class. She is also a travel agent and booked my flight to Ethiopia when I went to Solomon's graduation. She has had a front row seat to all of our adventures for several years now, so I felt comfortable calling her. She answered the phone and I said, "Hello, Sabrina, I know this is crazy, but I think the Lord just told me to get everything ready, because Solomon is coming here next Wednesday. Can you look into the flight options and prices, so we can start the process? I am not 100% sure, and I am concerned that this just may be my own mind telling me what my heart is yearning for, but we can at least check into it, in case it really is HIM."

She actually started to laugh, because she had been a witness to many of these experiences already. So she said all right then, let's get ready! I wanted to go to Washington, DC to greet Solomon when he landed on US soil. I was concerned he might get lost in customs and making the connecting flight to Raleigh. As it turned out, it was going to cost $1,000 for my ticket and we didn't have it.

Suddenly, Sabrina got excited when she realized her sister-in-law Heather was currently in Addis Ababa, Ethiopia, with her church from Tennessee, doing missions work. They work with the orphans in Korah, which is the dump in Addis Ababa.

Their team was already scheduled on the Wednesday flight from Ethiopia. What were the odds of there even being a flight on Wednesday, because they didn't have flights every day? Then to have Sabrina's sister-in-law on that flight was even more surreal. We began to pray right then that the Lord would orchestrate everything so that Solomon would not be alone, and could, in fact, fly with Heather as his escort.

A few days earlier, my friend Amy, in Fort Worth, Texas, whom I met through our blog and Kolfe Mama Ministry, had been reading the blog and said if Solomon's visa was approved, she wanted to pay for his plane ticket. I was shocked. I had never met her in person and was surprised by her offer. I had never told anyone we didn't have the money for his ticket. It is amazing to me how the Lord has used the blog to birth our ministry and to connect us with many like-minded people around the world.

After I hung up with Sabrina, I sent Amy an e-mail saying, "I think the Lord just told me that Solomon is coming next Wednesday. I was wondering if you were still interested in paying for his ticket. My husband is still unemployed at this time, and we would really appreciate your help if it still works out for you." She responded within minutes with a definite yes. I gave her Sabrina's telephone number and the two of them made all the arrangements to process the ticket.

Then I sent an e-mail to Solomon. It said, "Solomon, I think God just told me you are coming here next Wednesday, so you have to get everything ready. Pack all of your things and take care of any business you have. You may want to say goodbye to some of your friends too. We have not heard from the Embassy yet, so this really might not happen. But I think this is what God told me, so we have to be ready. I will be in touch as soon as we hear from the Embassy, which we hope will be any day." I also told him about Heather being there and possibly being his escort.

So now we had the trip tentatively planned for Wednesday, the ticket paid for, a possible escort, and we were in the waiting zone again. It had been three weeks since Solomon's Embassy appointment and we still had no word from them. Sabrina started calling every day to see if we had heard anything.

It was Monday morning. Jerry had gone to his 6 a.m. men's Bible study and I decided to stay in bed and cuddle with the kids. They love to cuddle in our bed and watch the PBS Kids morning programs. I was very tired and I just wanted to rest. When Jerry got home, we were still lying in bed at 9:16 a.m., when the phone rang with our regular call from Sabrina to see if we had heard from the Embassy. She said if we hadn't heard from them by noon that day, she would have to pull the hold on the ticket and Solomon would not make that flight. Jerry and I looked at each other and said if it is God's will, it will happen. I decided it was time to get the show on the road and start making beds.

Then at exactly 10:16, the phone rang again. This time Jerry answered and his voice sounded different. "Yes, this is the Mestas' residence. Yes, one moment, my wife is right here." He handed me the phone saying, "It is the US Embassy in Ethiopia!" I started to tremble as I reached for the phone. I sat back down on my bed and Jerry hushed the five 'littles' out of the room.

Then I heard, "Hello, this is Jeff at the US Embassy in Addis Ababa, Ethiopia. First, I would like to explain that I am very impressed by the amount of congressional interest there has been in this case. I want you to know we have a good reason for the delay of this case, as it is very unusual. I would like to interview you and get some more information, please." I was shocked that I was actually on the phone with the US Embassy in Ethiopia and then I thought, *Oh, no, I hope they are not mad at us for all the contacts from the Senator's office we initiated. They are probably calling to tell us he is denied.* Then he explained that he had actually interviewed Solomon at his Embassy appointment three weeks ago, and could not approve the visa then because of the unique circumstances involved. He said, "I am very puzzled by this whole situation. He is an orphan, and there is a lot of money being put up for him. How did you even meet him and why are you willing to go to such extremes for him? I need to verify that this is not just a back door adoption."

I took a deep breath and said, "Well, I would love to explain this situation to you, but it is going to take a little while. Do you have time right now? This is an amazing story of many miracles and I know it is very unique." He said yes, so I began to tell him the story. I told him how God dragged us to Kolfe, with me kicking and praying for Ryan Brown's plans to be thwarted that day. I told him about our visit, and how to this day I still don't have words to describe what God did to me, to Solomon, and our family.

I shared how Solomon had become the valedictorian of his school after failing the national exam, and how I had attended his graduation ceremony. I explained that God told me to go to Southeastern and ask for a scholarship for him, and all the miracles that we have experienced along the way. "Everyone has told us that the US Embassy will never approve his visa for international student status because he is an orphan and cannot prove he is going to return to his country after he graduates. But I need to tell you that I believe with everything in my being that God has handpicked Solomon for such a time as this. He has given him all these miracles in the last two years. I believe it is God's will that he study at SEBTS to be a pastor or missionary to minister to the orphan crisis in Ethiopia. Solomon wants them to hear his testimony and to know that God has not forgotten them. He has a plan and a future and hope for him, and we have been praying for this next miracle."

I barely got the last word out of my mouth when he replied, "Eileen, let me tell you something. My office closed over thirty minutes ago. I have been sitting here for the past hour, listening to the most amazing story I have ever heard. I am telling you that I am approving this visa right now!!!!" I literally started to scream and cry, and yelled down the hallway for the kids to hear, "PRAISE THE LORD! SOLOMON'S VISA IS APPROVED!! THANK YOU, JESUS, THANK YOU, LORD!"

I was jumping up and down, screaming and crying into the phone. I was so overwhelmed and jumping so hard that I literally wet my pants. The kids were all screaming and jumping right there with me, and could not believe their eyes when they saw Mama make pee-pee right there on the floor. Neither could Jerry or I, for that matter! I was wiping my legs with my nightgown and Jerry ran for a towel to help me. The kids were wide-eyed and laughing as the typical commotion was going on.

Then I heard Jeff saying, "Okay, now I just have to get a few more details and fill out some forms, while I have you on the line. I am going to process this visa right now and I will call Solomon tomorrow to arrange for him to pick it up." Just then I remembered about his flight and I said, "Oh, no, oh, wait, I know this is crazy, but God told me he was coming here this Wednesday, and we already have his flight tentatively booked. Can you call him right now, because his flight is tentatively booked to fly out tomorrow night?"

He said, "Eileen, it is 7:30 at night here and my wife is waiting for me outside. I really need to go now."

So I said, "Can I call Solomon right now and tell him?"

He said, "Sure, go ahead and tell him to be here first thing in the morning to pick up his visa. He can get it and then fly out tomorrow night. I also wrote a note on his paperwork that he was coming early to attend a Bible school in Tennessee, which will explain why he is arriving earlier than SEBTS matriculation starts. This should prevent any problems with customs."

We hung up the phone and immediately called Sabrina to book that ticket!! She was screaming and crying now too. I got some composure, took a quick shower and then got on the computer to place a Skype call to Solomon. Of course, it was in the middle of the night for him, so we woke him up again. When I told him we had just gotten off the phone with the Embassy and they approved his visa, he started to laugh and cry at the same time.

He was elated and could not believe it. He said he felt like he was living in a dream. I told him he had to be at the Embassy first thing in the morning to get his visa, and then he had to call Heather, Sabrina's sister-in-law, to make plans to meet them to go to the airport. They had never actually met, but we had been communicating about this for several days now. Heather and some of their church members had also been reading our blog and had known Solomon's story for some time. We all never imagined that the Lord would orchestrate her to be his personal escort.

Solomon arrived at the Embassy first thing Tuesday morning and the guard would not let him in, because his name was not on the roster for an appointment. He explained that he was told to come pick up his visa, but the guard said they only issue visas on

Wednesday. Solomon tried to explain again and the guard said he must leave immediately. Thank God he had a cell phone, because he called us right away. It was the middle of the night for us now. He was very upset, saying the guard would not listen to him or even let him speak. We told him to just wait there and we would call him back.

Jerry remembered Jeff's name and got on the US Embassy Ethiopia website to find their direct telephone number. We called for thirty minutes, but there was no answer. Finally, we got through to his office and he got on the line. I explained that Solomon was waiting down on the street because the guard would not let him in to pick up his visa. He started to laugh and said not to worry, that he would take care of it. We called Solomon, and awhile later he called back to tell us a lady came outside and handed him his visa. What a day! He was now on his way to meet with Heather and the team from Tennessee. They planned to take him to dinner before they headed to the airport.

During all this excitement I heard the Lord whisper, *"I want you to tell this story. Call the newspaper and the news channel to be at the airport."* Earlier, our local newspaper, the *Wake Weekly*, had printed a very nice story about our family and ministry to the Kolfe Boys Orphanage, which included Solomon's story. So, I sent an e-mail telling them Solomon was arriving at the airport that very afternoon. I suggested they do part three of this story, since they had already done a two-part miniseries.

Also, earlier that summer, I had met a reporter from the local ABC News station when our three-year-olds were playing together in our community pool. I sent her an e-mail and she remembered me. I wrote a bio about Solomon and suggested they send a reporter to be at the airport for his arrival.

During this waiting zone, I had also been praying to have at least 100 people for his homecoming. Within an hour of sending the e-mails, they both responded yes. ABC News and the local paper were sending reporters to cover this story. We were sending e-mails and Facebook blasts, asking everyone to come to the airport to welcome him home. We were not sure if word was getting out in time, but we trusted the Lord for the outcome.

We got word that Solomon was, in fact, on the flight to the

USA, and then the call "The eagle has landed" came when he was in DC. We were on cloud nine, and rushing to make posters, gather balloons, etc. for our trek to the airport. Then we got the call that "Solomon was missing!" When the group got to customs, they were separated because he was not an American. They were sent in two different directions. Heather called to tell us the team was out looking for him. One of them said, "We just spent sixteen hours talking with this kid and he is pretty smart. He is probably sitting in the gateway for his flight to Raleigh already." When they got to the terminal to check, he was sitting there with his papers and bags in hand. There is nothing like suspense and excitement to keep your heart pumping!

Heather gave him her cell to call me and I could not believe my precious boy was really here in America. I told him that he needed to go wash up really good; because as soon as he got off the plane in Raleigh, there was a crowd of 100 people waiting for him, and the television news and local newspaper reporters were going to interview him. I told him to think about what he was going to say and get ready. I didn't want him to be so surprised that he was speechless.

So there we were at RDU Airport on a Wednesday morning in June 2010, with only a twenty-four hour notice to prepare. All of our family and friends, totaling approximately 100 people, came marching into the terminal with banners, posters, and balloons to welcome Solomon to the USA. I never saw so many balloons at the airport. We were so excited. The reporters interviewed us before he arrived, and then suddenly, what we had prayed about for three years became a reality! Solomon came walking out of the terminal, and the crowd roared and cheered and cried and clapped and jumped up and down with joy, as we witnessed a life-changing miracle. We ran to him and he dropped his bags and started to hug and kiss us, and he burst into tears! His knees were weak and he just melted into our arms.

The ABC News cameras were rolling and the reporter put the microphone right in his face and started to interview him. The first thing she asked was, "What do you think of this lady right here?" pointing to me, "And how do you describe what she means to you?" I fell apart when he said, "SHE GAVE ME MY LIFE!"

There are no real words to describe how I felt. I had prayed and ached for this precious boy for so long and I could feel my heart pounding against my rib cage. Again, I was thinking back on the day when I did not want to even visit the Kolfe Boys Orphanage. I stand in awe of how little control I have over what God has planned for my life. Look what "I" would have missed!

As God would have it, Solomon got here on Wednesday and Jerry got a new job on Thursday. It was clear that God again proved we could take no credit for making this dream a reality! But now that he was finally here, we did need a job to be able to feed and care for him. God's timing is always perfect and He is so good!

24 The Unexpected Surprises

The first morning Solomon was with us, I made a huge breakfast feast while the kids were setting the table. I turned on the radio to hear worship music and to my surprise, the song "You're Not Alone" by Meredith Andrews had just started to play. She is a beautiful Christian singing artist who won a Dove Award for her music. We met Meredith a few years ago at an orphan conference where we were speaking and she was leading worship, and we have since become friends. I told her all about Solomon and how we had dedicated her song to him. She autographed a CD that we sent him for Christmas, with a two-fold dedication. The words are absolutely beautiful, describing that God is always with us; and we also added the truth that, because we are now his unofficially adopted family, he was no longer alone. He often wrote and told me he listened to it every night before he went to bed, and one day he asked how she knew what was in his heart to write about it. That morning, I blasted the radio as loud as it would go so everyone in the house could hear it. What were the odds that our theme song would be playing the very first time I turned on the radio with Solomon in our house!? I literally looked up to the heavens, saying, "Lord, your attention to every little detail in our lives is amazing!"

Two days later, we packed up the van and drove Solomon and Ellie, with other friends of hers, to Chattanooga, Tennessee Precept Ministry Bible Study Boot Camp. They would be there for the next week. Kay Arthur even made a point to personally visit with Solomon while he was there. He impressed everyone with his soccer skills and already started making new friends, while learning the Scriptures.

Our five 'littles' were absolutely precious when they saw

Solomon for the first time in person. They had only seen photos and talked to him on Skype. They too had been praying for three years and witnessed the miracles on this journey. They felt like he was their long lost brother who was finally home. You would have never known Solomon was our newbie.

After boot camp, we spent the next few weeks adjusting to his new life and our family. We were intentionally seeking to make him feel loved and welcomed. We went to the community pool every day and I told him he had to learn to swim because this was a life skill. He worked hard and learned within a month. He was my boy and I treated him the same as all my other children. We give lots of hugs and kisses, along with chores and responsibilities, to serve and care for each other as a family unit. We were being intentional to disciple him and integrate him into our family and a new culture.

We took a family vacation to the beach for some much needed rest and relaxation. He saw the ocean for the first time in his life and he loved riding the waves on the boogie board. He said he had no idea the ocean was so strong and powerful. Everything he did and ate was a first for him, even though he was nineteen years old. We were getting to experience many firsts with him, just like with all of our children, and we were so happy. He was now with his family in America who loved him; he had his own room, good nutritious food readily available, and his favorite strawberry ice cream always in the freezer. He started school in August and seemed to be doing very well. His English still needed a lot of work and we were intentionally trying to help him with everything we could. We had great excitement and anticipation for his future.

One afternoon, I heard on the radio that Meredith Andrews was coming to Raleigh. I sent her an e-mail telling her Solomon was finally here and we wanted to see her. A few days later, we were with Meredith as she was performing a live concert for HIS radio. She was so happy to see Solomon and he could not believe he was meeting her in person. When she started to sing "You're Not Alone" she said, "Solomon, this is for you!" We stood there with our arms around each other and then he lost it. He started to cry and buried his head in my chest as we wept together. Meredith was watching us and then she too burst into tears. She couldn't finish singing and said, "I'm sorry, folks, but I just need to tell you about my friends here. Eileen and Solomon, will you please come up here?"

We walked up and huddled together in tears. Then she asked us to share our story with the audience, so I shared a brief testimony about Solomon. What was the chance that Solomon had spent the last year in an orphanage in Ethiopia, listening to this song every night before he went to sleep, and now he was standing right here in America, with Meredith singing it to him live? What an amazing God we serve. Only He could have orchestrated this. There was not a dry eye in the house. The HIS Radio DJ asked us to do a personal interview that was aired on the radio.

A few weeks later, we were again at a concert, this time it was the Chapman Family Tour with Steven Curtis and Mary Beth Chapman. We have developed a friendship with them as well, since our involvement with their ministry, Show Hope. They invited us backstage to visit after the concert. They too were so excited to see the miraculous arrival of Solomon.

Then five months later, in November 2010, exactly one year from the time we started the process to bring Solomon to the US, we drove to Hershey, Pennsylvania to speak at the Mid-Atlantic Orphan Summit. There were more than 500 people at this conference. I was one of the plenary speakers on Friday night and Dr. Russell Moore, who was speaking after me, was in the front row, hearing our testimony. He is the author of the Southern Baptist Convention's resolution stating it is the church's responsibility to care for orphans that I quoted to help get Solomon's scholarship at SEBTS. He also wrote the book, *Adopted For Life,* that I highly recommend. Although we had met before, how incredible that he would be sitting in the front row, hearing our testimony of how the Lord made fruit from his labor? As I shared our testimony, Solomon was also in the front row to hear it all for the first time. When I finished speaking, instead of pointing to the usual video that showed our visit to Kolfe, I asked Solomon to please stand and introduced him. The audience had no idea he was going to be there. There were gasps of surprise and people crying as they gave him a standing ovation! The dream I'd had exactly one year ago in November 2009, just before we had started his journey to America came true! Later, Meredith Andrews, who ironically led worship for the conference, sang "You're Not Alone" live to Solomon again. This time she finished the song without breaking down.

In January 2011, Solomon and I were invited to visit my friend Amy and her family in Fort Worth, Texas. I was excited to finally meet her in person and thank her for paying for Solomon's plane ticket. This is also the home of the Gladney Center for Adoptions headquarters. We were invited to visit the Gladney campus and it was the first time for both of us. Our adoption process was done online and via telephone conversations. Scott Brown invited us to share our testimony with the staff, and we were blessed to see Ryan and Abby Brown again, who just happened to be visiting in town that weekend. How amazing to come full circle with Gladney and Ryan Brown, who were the very people responsible for exposing the Kolfe Boys Orphanage to the world, and for taking us there kicking and screaming, which eventually resulted in Solomon coming to the USA. He is no longer a forgotten and hopeless orphan boy. None of us ever expected to be all together, standing on USA soil at the Gladney headquarters, for such a time as this. It was another surreal and amazing experience. I kept telling him I was amazed at how the Lord was orchestrating so many divine appointments for him to meet so many people who had played a role in our journey to him. It was unbelievable. Amy also arranged for us to share our testimony at five additional events that weekend, with the hope of encouraging more people to get involved in adoption and orphan care.

Solomon was spending his time going to school and studying. Fortunately, he was only gone for a few hours four days a week, so his schedule was not that hectic. He seemed to be doing well at first. When I would ask questions about school or if he needed help, he would always say everything was fine and he didn't need any help. One day he told me he wanted us to stop teaching him English because he would get the hang of it by himself. He started to spend more time in his room and began to withdraw from spending time with us. He would join us at mealtime and hardly look at anyone or speak, and then withdraw to his room.

He preferred to be in his room and on his computer. He was not happy with some of our rules, like having to keep his door open while he was on the computer. I was concerned that he was getting depressed for his homeland, and knew he needed time and space to adjust. We intentionally tried not to pressure him, but we also wanted to include him in our family and build healthy hedges of protection. I knew he was used to being alone and not having any accountability, so I was praying for wisdom on a daily basis.

He was playing soccer at school and making friends who were inviting him to go out to eat, to the movies, and to fellowship with them. He was learning so many new things about our culture and about being part of a family. His chores were to empty the dishwasher every day, help set the table for meals, and keep his room clean. Every day I was in awe and could not believe he was really here with us. Sometimes, he would come out of his room, and I would jokingly look at him with surprise, saying, "Hey, who are you and how did you get here?" Then I would give him a big hug and kiss and tell him how much I loved him. I kept reminding him of all the miracles God had performed in his life, and told him daily that I was so proud of him for working so hard at school, and so grateful he was with us. I told him every single day that God had great plans for him.

We had a wonderful Thanksgiving and Christmas celebration. We taught him about traditions and the intentional focus of keeping Christ in all of them. He enjoyed decorating the Christmas tree and having his own special ornament to hang. He loved baking all the cookies, the food, and putting up all the lights and decorations. He was very excited when it snowed and we went sleigh-riding and built snowmen. We included him in everything, from making crafts to cooking, and shopping and wrapping gifts. I even taught him how to bake a cake. I was having so much fun watching him grow and learn so many new things. It is our homeschool motto to learn something new every day and he fit right in.

In March, we took another family vacation, this time to Disney World in Florida. I often joke that if you are born in New York you have to die in Florida, because the majority of my relatives now live there. We had a wonderful time with family who were finally meeting Solomon in person. The 'littles' were bursting with energy and excitement to see all the Disney characters. They loved the parade, the castle, and train rides. We told them they could have only one souvenir, and we were shocked when our three little boys unanimously agreed they wanted a print of Abraham Lincoln from the Hall of Presidents exhibit. We had studied about him in school and expressed how grateful we are for his faithfulness and love of God. His role in history directly impacted our ability to be a multiracial family today! We never expected our little guys to have such a love for him as well, especially while having so many other options at Disney World. During our three days there, Solomon hardly spoke a word. He seemed to enjoy himself, but we were all puzzled by his withdrawn and quiet behavior. When we asked him if he was having fun, he said yes, without any emotion or excitement. Again, we were concerned that there was something wrong, but didn't want to put any pressure on him, so we just gave him space. He was always a man of few words and would not open up to us.

Because of our involvement in the orphan ministry, I had learned that many children who come from orphanages suffer from RAD. *Reactive Attachment Disorder (RAD)* is a mental health disorder in which a child is unable to form healthy social relationships, particularly with a primary caregiver. Often children with RAD will seem charming and helpless to outsiders, while waging a campaign of terror within the family. RAD is frequently seen in children who have had inconsistent or abusive care in early childhood, including children adopted from orphanages or foster care. Solomon was displaying many of the symptoms. He would act fine in front of other people, but when we were home he would be withdrawn and want to stay in his room alone. So I began to pray for wisdom and started to pursue getting counseling. I talked to him about it, but he would not engage in conversation with me. I began feeling tremendous stress and a huge responsibility to give him more of my time and attention. I wanted him to be happy and succeed. He started to act like 'the honeymoon was over,' and became very irritable, withdrawn, and even sarcastic. I was worried about him.

I shared my concerns with Jerry, our pastor, and my girlfriends, who I affectionately call my 'sistahs,' because they are my spiritual sisters who I know will give wise biblical counsel to me when I need it. They are gifts from the Lord and I cherish them. I told them I felt like we were under a severe spiritual attack and described it like a dark cloud was hovering over our home. I began feeling tension in my marriage, and was very stressed and irritable, and cried out to the Lord for wisdom and discernment. I prayed for revelation and intervention to bring an end to this darkness and oppression. I was asking for wisdom on how to help him open up and succeed.

I also noticed Solomon started to act more aggressively affectionate toward me in an inappropriate way. Jerry and Ellie also noticed it and mentioned their concern. He was not the same, and I couldn't figure out what was going on. No matter how much I tried, he would not communicate with me and preferred to withdraw. Then in May 2011, all heck broke loose when we discovered that Solomon had been intentionally hiding his cell phone in the bathroom to record our family. We were heartbroken, shocked, and devastated. We had a friend come immediately to counsel and question him, and he confessed to recording more than sixty times in the past month. He also admitted that I was his primary target and that he had developed inappropriate feelings toward me. Within a few hours of finding out he was recording us, he had to leave our home, and some friends of ours agreed to house him while we sorted things out. This was not at all what we had expected this journey to look like only eleven months later. It became evident that it was not healthy, safe, or possible for him to stay with us any longer.

I felt betrayed, violated, angry, and like I was having a nervous breakdown. I was angry that my family had been violated. I didn't understand why this had happened and I felt like a failure. I was also grieving the loss of my boy Solomon. I honestly thought Solomon would forever be in our family. He was legally too old to be adopted, but we believed the Lord had brought him into our family, and we adopted him into our hearts as our son. We didn't need legal documents. I was suddenly thrust into a new situation that I didn't know how to handle! My dreams for my son Solomon were crushed. Our relationship was never going to be the same. I could not believe how much he had changed and how he had been acting out. I needed some time to reflect and pray for wisdom, healing, compassion, and forgiveness.

I believe Satan got a foothold by tempting Solomon and getting him off-track. He tried to destroy us and our ministry in orphan care. The Holy Spirit was alerting me that there was evil lurking in our home. God knew this was happening and He answered my prayer by faithfully revealing it, and protecting us from it getting worse. Nothing happens in this world without God allowing it, like He teaches us in the book of Job! *"The thief comes only to steal and kill and destroy; I have come that they may have life, and have it to the full" (John 10:10).*

I have learned so much through this experience about the heart of God, the pain and suffering of orphans, and about grace and forgiveness. We knew bringing Solomon into our home at nineteen years of age was a risk, but we also knew the Lord orchestrated every detail to make it happen. We walked by faith. Just because things didn't turn out the way we thought does not mean God wasn't in it, or that we did something wrong. We had no control of Solomon's choices. We could not force him to want what God offered him, but we can choose to forgive, love, and pray for him. I heard so many unsuccessful stories of older child adoptions, and I hoped and prayed that our story with Solomon would be different. It is true that older children come from very hard places and they are wounded and broken. Honestly, they are really just like the rest of us sinners, but they do need extra help, hope, love, patience, forgiveness, and lots of counseling. Although we tried to help Solomon, we could not force him to get counseling and do what was right. Because he was with us as an international student and not legally adopted, we had no legal rights to make him do anything. He did not want to get counseling and work toward healing and reconciliation. He denied that there was a problem and said he just wanted to leave.

Solomon left our home in May 2011, and went to live with people in New York that he met when they visited Kolfe before he came to live with us. They also had another boy from Kolfe with them as an international student, and were able to enroll Solomon in a computer school. We don't know them and they have never communicated with us. I would periodically send him an e-mail message that I was praying for him and that we all loved and missed him, but he would not respond. I asked him to let us help him build a healthy relationship again, but he did not want to. He said he wanted to move on with his new life and told me he did not want anything to do with us anymore. He literally cut off all communication with us. I continued to pray the Lord would heal him and give us complete restoration someday.

More than a year passed and on September 14, 2012, I was elated to receive an e-mail from Solomon. He attached a photo of us together in Ethiopia and said:

This picture makes me cry all day long. Hope you all doing well. You was truly a great mom. Thank you for everything. I am going back to Ethiopia soon. I got a congratulation letter from school today. The letter is about my 4.0 first year achievement. I am so happy for that. I made a lot of connection with a lot of people here in New York. So, I am gonna' go back and reapply for other school. I already got sponsor and a family to live with. I am so blessed. I loved you all so much. I am following your blog even if I didn't e-mail to you guys. Things always happen for a good reason. My life is changed dramatically. God is so good. But I never forget that you are the reason for all of this. So I am always grateful for that. Please tell Ellie to study hard for the nursing school. I also happy for Melissa and Randy for their third child. BJ also in the military so, tell him to be careful. I am so proud of you and papa for your obedience to God. Tell all the littles I love them so much. I wish if I was there and helping you folding all those closes on the couch. Lol

Thank you so much for all your sweet word. I am so glad that I terminated from Southeastern and came to New York. I would be so sad if I went back without living here in New York. I spent the whole year in North Carolina without having a friend. I am not ready to be so religious, in fact my religion is so much different than protestant. Honestly I hated to go to church and Southeastern school, but I didn't have any choice back then. I wasn't happy when we talked in Texas. I didn't like when we went to Hershey Pennsylvania. I know you believe that God did this and that but that is your opinion. God never talked me or nothing. If he talked you or say something to you that's your story. I have different faith and religion so, it was so hard for me to accept everything that you said. Any way mom, you might not heard from me again but I want you to know that I am not completely gone from your life. Your help and all those good times remain in my heart forever.

I love you all,
Solomon

His original visa was approved for two years and was specifically associated with SEBTS. When he requested an extension with the new school, the US Immigration Department decided not to renew his visa status, and said he must leave the country immediately. I am so grateful that he decided to reconcile with us before he had to leave, and that we are able to communicate again. I know, that I know, that I know, that he is in God's hands and He is trustworthy to continue to care for him. God created him, He knows how many hairs are on his head, and He has a plan for a good future and hope for Solomon's life. I have no doubt that God parted the seas and created every opportunity for him to come to the USA specifically to study at SEBTS, regardless of what he thinks. God had a plan for him to be here for such a time as this, but he didn't want what He had prepared for him to do. I continue to pray for Solomon every day and I have no regrets. I love him and pray for complete healing in his life. I especially pray that he will come to know the truth that life is about a "relationship with Jesus Christ," and not religion. They are two very different things. God gives us all a choice to choose Him or not. Solomon has clearly communicated his choice.

As I cried out to the Lord for wisdom on why and what happened, He took me to Nehemiah 9. God performed so many miracles to set His people free from slavery in Egypt, and yet they quickly departed from Him. He saw their sufferings and heard their cry. He sent miraculous signs and wonders against Pharaoh, He parted the sea; by day He guided them with a pillar of cloud, and by night with a pillar of fire, to give them light on the way they were to take. He came down on Mount Sinai and He spoke to them from heaven. He gave regulations and laws that are just and right, and decrees and commands that are good. In their hunger He dropped bread and meat from heaven, and in their thirst He brought water from the rock. He gave His good Spirit to instruct them.

But they became arrogant and stiff-necked and did not obey His commands. They refused to listen and failed to remember the miracles He performed among them. They became rebellious and appointed a leader in order to return to their slavery. But He is a forgiving God; gracious and compassionate, slow to anger, and abounding in love. Therefore He did not desert them, even when they cast for themselves an image of a calf and said, "This is our God who brought us out of Egypt," or when they committed awful blasphemies. For forty years He sustained them in the desert; they lacked nothing, their clothes did not wear out, nor did their feet become swollen. He gave them kingdoms and many children. But there was a consequence to the generation that would not obey the Lord. They were not permitted to enter the Promised Land.

It was only when they had all died off that the next generation was permitted to receive the blessing and enter the Promised Land. He protected them from their enemies, and when they took possession of the new land they were given houses filled with all kinds of good things: wells already dug, vineyards, olive groves, and fruit trees in abundance. They ate to the full and were well-nourished; they reveled in His great goodness. But then they became disobedient and rebelled against God too. They put His law behind their backs, killed His prophets who admonished them in order to turn them back to God, and they committed awful blasphemies. So He handed them over to their enemies, who oppressed them. When they were oppressed, they cried out to God again. And He heard them from heaven, and in His great compassion He gave them deliverers, who rescued them from the hand of their enemies. God delivered them time after time.

They wanted their own way and what they thought to be the better. God had a plan to give them freedom and blessings in the new land, but they did not want to do things His way. Throughout the Scriptures we learn how people fall into temptation and sin, and miss what God had planned for them. But even though they rebelled against God; in His mercy, He remained faithful to call them back to Himself, continuing to give them opportunities to repent and get back on track. He is a loving God who forgives and restores broken lives. His mercies are new every morning. He desires that none should perish and that all would walk in truth, righteousness, and holiness. He allows free will, but with consequences and/or blessings, all for the purpose of calling all of us into a love relationship with Him.

As I was writing this book, I really prayed about what to include in tHIS story. I struggled with whether or not I should share about the sin and hard things that we have gone through. And then I heard that whisper from the Lord, *"Eileen, have you not read My book? It is full of stories about real people with real experiences of the good, the bad, and the ugly! This is not a prosperity gospel, this is all about Me doing a work with sinners like you and it is for*

My Glory!"

Just look at David and Moses, who both murdered people, yet they were still greatly used by God because they repented and surrendered their lives to Him. There are stories of prostitutes, incest, lies, kidnapping, and all kinds of immoral behavior. Sin and bad things happen to people and there is nothing new under the sun. Satan doesn't want people to talk about him and how he operates. The truth is, especially when we are on the front lines in ministry, living and working for God, Satan is always on the attack to discourage and distract us from God's plan. Many times when things don't go the way we plan, and people don't know the truth of God's Word that gives us wisdom and faith to trust Him no matter what happens; they often become afraid, angry, and rebellious, and then retreat and turn their backs on God.

This situation had a major impact on our family and could have destroyed our ministry. I am sure reading this chapter has even made you feel discouraged. But I know that God has a purpose in allowing this to happen, and I will trust HIM no matter what! We all need to know how Satan works, so that we are empowered to fight the good fight and not to be discouraged by his attacks. We all had to work through the process of forgiveness as well. *"... Forgive, and you will be forgiven" (Luke 6:37)*. Forgiveness doesn't mean what's been done to you is okay. It means you surrender it to God, for He is faithful to carry out justice. We give up the right to get revenge or harbor bitterness. We will all answer to Him for what we do. It is also important to understand that everything we do affects other people, either as a blessing or a curse. Everything we do impacts the Kingdom of God. I will speak of the good, the bad, and the ugly things that happened, because God is at work in all of it, even when it doesn't make sense and we don't understand. He is writing this story, not me! I am just taking everything He has given me to deal with and sharing my testimony of faith and how He carries me through it all. That is how we encourage each other to remain faithful, no matter what trials or blessings may come.

I believe it is important to be transparent and communicate the truth and reality of what we experienced. Taking in an older orphan is a challenge, a risk, can be dangerous; and requires a calling, a deep faith and relationship with God, along with a great support group. It means you have to trust God no matter what happens, and know that He is in control. It means you might get hurt. I have a little more wisdom from my personal experience to share about some behavioral things to watch out for. There is a lot of credibility when someone has personally experienced something, compared to just speculating. I don't believe everyone will have a bad experience. In fact, I do have friends who have had great experiences with older child adoptions. It may be difficult, but not impossible, to have a success story. But not everyone will have the same story. I will never tell anyone not to adopt an older child, which is what Satan wanted me to do. I will still encourage people to adopt and care for older orphans, because God calls us to and they are worth fighting for! I pray that this testimony will help others be informed, as well as be encouraged, if God is calling them to adopt an older child. He is faithful and will carry you through it all, the good, the bad, and the ugly! God is still writing Solomon's story and I am praying he will continue to communicate with us and forever be in our lives.

Although this turned out to be more than "I" could handle, the Lord faithfully carried me through the darkness and despair of this last year. I have repented for my anger, and asked Solomon for forgiveness for my initial outburst of anger toward him. I have been refreshed and encouraged by the Lord, His Holy Word, family, and the many saints who were on the front lines with us, praying for Solomon and holding us up. Many of these people are friends through the Christian Alliance for Orphans ministry and I am forever grateful to all of them. God faithfully uses His people to accomplish His will and carry us through the darkness of trials, if we are faithful to trust and call out to them for help. This is how the body of Christ is supposed to work. I know that nothing is impossible with God, and He has the power to take these ashes and turn them into beauty in Solomon's life. I still have great excitement, hope, and anticipation that God is going to use Solomon for great things and for His Glory! And I pray that you will be encouraged by tHIS story to be faithful, no matter what you may be going through in your own life.

This is one of my prayers for Solomon:

I have not stopped giving thanks for you, remembering you in my prayers. I keep asking that the God of our Lord Jesus Christ, the glorious Father, may give you the Spirit of wisdom and revelation, so that you may know him better. I pray also that the eyes of your heart may be enlightened in order that you may know the hope to which he has called you, the riches of his glorious inheritance in the saints, and his incomparably great power for us who believe ... (Ephesians 1:16-19).

25 Answer the Call

Throughout Scripture, I have learned about people who lived by faith and not by sight. They endured persecution, many hardships and trials, as well as miracles and blessings. I see people of faith who heard the voice of God telling them to do things that seemed impossible, and often not popular in their culture. They had to make a choice to obey or not. This has brought me much comfort as I too have stepped out in faith to the call of the Lord on my life

Look at Noah, who by faith obeyed God when He told him to build a huge boat in the middle of the desert, where there was no water in sight! He told him to prepare for a flood, which didn't make any sense. Noah's life called for major adjustments to be obedient. Everyone thought he was a crazy man; they scoffed at him and mocked him ... until the rains came down and flooded the earth. He and his family were the only survivors, along with the animals that walked onto the boat by God's command. He didn't have to go hunt them down and drag them into the boat, they all just miraculously showed up, in pairs, male and female! *Now faith is the substance of things hoped for, the evidence of things not seen (Hebrews 11:1 KJV)*. Noah hoped he had heard God correctly, and they were on that boat for a long time, more than forty days and nights. They probably wondered if they would even survive, and questioned why God was doing this. I imagine the odor of animals and unsanitary conditions had to be horrible. They endured much hardship and could not see what the future was going to bring. Then finally, one day, the rains stopped! Noah, his family, and all the animals were finally on dry land and God blessed them. He gave them instructions on what to do. He told them to *be fruitful and increase in number and fill the earth. And from each man, too, I will demand an accounting for the life of his fellow man (Genesis 9:1, 5).* The adventure was over and now it was time to get to the work of restoring the earth for the next 350 years, and then Noah died at the age of 950. He lived a long life of being about the Lord's business.

God called Abraham to leave Mesopotamia and go to Canaan. He had a comfortable life that suddenly ended when God decided it was time for him to move on to the next purpose for his life. With total obedience, he moved his family to the land of promise and a new life, even though he had no idea where, why, or what was going to happen. All he knew was that God was telling him to go! When God calls someone to make life adjustments, we just have to do it. His wife Sarah was not able to have children, but somehow God had convinced Abraham that this was temporary. As she grew older, both Abraham and Sarah had doubt, and decided to take matters into their own hands with Hagar, which backfired on them. Like us, they were not perfect, and they made many mistakes out of fear and selfish desires along the way. They endured much hardship during the wait. They suffered a famine and many other trials. But in His perfect timing, God finally decided to bless them with a son, Isaac, in their old age. Then one day God told Abraham to bind Isaac and take him to the mount to be offered as a sacrifice. I'm sure he wondered if he had heard God right, and he must have had many questions, like "Why did You perform all these miracles and give him to me, only to sacrifice him now?" Although filled with doubt, he obeyed God, and when God saw his obedience, He called out to him; and provided the sacrifice of a ram found in the thicket, and Isaac was released. God tested Abraham and he proved faithful. Abraham's life was full of trials and suffering while he was walking in obedience to God's call, and He was faithful to never leave his side. From the day God called Abraham to leave his home until his last hour, he walked every suffering in joyful obedience to God's desire for him. God is the same today as He was then. As I sit here today, still grieving the loss of our Solomon, and still being in great financial debt from being out of work for three years; though I don't understand it all, I find comfort knowing that God is still in control and He has a plan. He desires that we walk by faith, not by sight, with obedience to answer His call and purpose, even when we don't understand it. He wants us to be His disciples and follow after Him.

The greatest role model of all is the life and death of Jesus Christ. Even He was guided by the voice of God and chose His will. When He was in the garden at Gethsemane, he went to pray. *"Abba, Father,"* ... *"everything is possible for you. Take this cup from me. Yet not what I will, but what you will" (Mark 14:36).* He asked Father God if it was possible not to have to die on the cross. But He was willing to do the will of God above His own desires. Jesus went to the cross to die for the sins of the world because He obeyed His heavenly Father to fulfill the prophecy.

"I am the good shepherd. The good shepherd lays down his life for the sheep. I am the good shepherd; I know my sheep and my sheep know me—just as the Father knows me and I know the Father—and I lay down my life for the sheep. I have other sheep that are not of this sheep pen. I must bring them also. They too will listen to my voice, and there shall be one flock and one shepherd. The reason my Father loves me is that I lay down my life—only to take it up again. No one takes it from me, but I lay it down of my own accord. I have authority to lay it down and authority to take it up again. This command I received from my Father" (John 10:11, 14-18). Jesus paid the price of His perfect, sinless life for our sins. He chose to obey the will of His Father and laid down His life of His own accord. He did it for the sheep; his people, the Jews, and the sheep not of this pen, the Gentiles. He adopted those outside of His pen as well.

Sin cannot enter into the holy place of heaven, so without a way to wash our sin, we would never be able to enter. Through receiving Him as our Savior, we are washed clean so that we can enter the holy kingdom of heaven for all eternity. What does this teach us about the value of human beings? Jesus demonstrates for us the value of every human being created by God. He gave His own life as the sacrifice for sinners. He wants that none should perish. There is no greater love than to sacrifice one's life for another.

My life too, has been a journey of walking in sin, repenting, growing in faith, going through trials, hardships and persecution, as well as miracles and blessings. The Lord gave me eight children to lay down my life for and to train up to know Him. It's a choice I make freely, and though I fall short every day, I pray for the faith, strength, and wisdom to finish the job well.

Praise be to the God and Father of our Lord Jesus Christ, who has blessed us in the heavenly realms with every spiritual blessing in Christ. For he chose us in him before the creation of the world to be holy and blameless in his sight. In love he predestined us to be adopted as his sons through Jesus Christ, in accordance with his pleasure and will—to the praise of his glorious grace, which he has freely given us in the One he loves. In him we have redemption through his blood, the forgiveness of sins, in accordance with the riches of God's grace that he lavished on us with all wisdom and understanding. And he made known to us the mystery of his will according to his good pleasure (Ephesians 1:3-9).

I have no doubt that each one of my children was predestined to be mine. I am forever grateful that I too was adopted into the family of God, when I understood and accepted that I was bought with the blood of Jesus Christ and asked Him to be my Savior. If you have surrendered your life to Jesus Christ as your personal Savior, then you are my sister or brother in Christ, and we are adopted into one family. Adoption was created by God and is the gospel of Jesus Christ.

Let us fix our eyes on Jesus, the author and perfecter of our faith, who for the joy set before him endured the cross, scorning its shame, and sat down at the right hand of the throne of God. Consider him who endured such opposition from sinful men, so that you will not grow weary and lose heart (Hebrews 12:2-3).

When the hard times come, let's fix our eyes on Jesus and remember what He did for us. Nothing compares to carrying the sins of the whole world and being crucified. If He did that for us, surely we can do whatever He calls us to do and endure suffering for Him to perfect our faith.

For it is by grace you have been saved, through faith—and this not from yourselves, it is the gift of God, not by works, so that no one can boast. For we are God's workmanship, created in Christ Jesus to do good works, which God prepared in advance for us to do (Ephesians 2:8-10). I have no doubt everything the Lord has done in my life was planned by Him for me to do. It has been so much more than I can handle, and it required Him to perform miracles, which proved I can take no credit for anything. I boast in Christ alone!

The Pharisees got together and asked Jesus, *"Teacher, which is the greatest commandment in the Law?" Jesus replied, "Love the Lord your God with all your heart and with all your soul and with all your mind. This is the first and greatest commandment"* (Matthew 22:36-38). ... *The LORD our God, the LORD is one. Love the LORD your God with all your heart and with all your soul and with all your strength. These commandments that I give you today are to be upon your hearts. Impress them on your children. Talk about them when you sit at home and when you walk along the road, when you lie down and when you get up (Deuteronomy 6:4-9).* God wants our whole heart and the hearts of our children to love and serve Him. He tells us to impress these commandments on the children. Our greatest commission is to lead the children to Christ, so we can enter together into the kingdom of heaven for all eternity. The family is the fundamental institution created by God. Children belong in families, not orphanages or the foster care system. Families are discipleship centers for transferring the relationship with Christ.

The home is the second greatest influence outside of the Holy Spirit. God gives authority and power to parents over the hearts of our children. He also gives a multi-generational vision and priority. *"... Repent and be baptized, every one of you, in the name of Jesus Christ for the forgiveness of your sins. And you will receive the gift of the Holy Spirit.* **The promise is for you and your children and for all who are far off***—for all whom the Lord our God will call"* (Acts 2:38-39, emphasis added). The gospel is all about a relationship with God, and the order of priority being for us, then our children, and then the world. Together with family and the church, we are to go make a difference for the Lord. *"Therefore, go and make disciples of all nations, baptizing them in the name of the Father and of the Son and of the Holy Spirit, and teaching them to obey everything I have commanded you. And surely I am with you always, to the very end of the age"* (Matthew 28:19). Jesus promises to be with us on this journey!

The latest statistic I read is that there are 163 million orphans on Planet Earth right now. These are children that are not in families and who are without the protection and training by parents, as commanded by the Lord. Without this covering of protection, they are Satan's prey. Satan has an agenda to attack the family and everything God has created for good. If we don't get involved in the lives of these children, they will be the next godless generation … no other options! Satan hasn't forgotten these children, and he wants to disrupt God's plans for world evangelism. His primary target is children!

Orphans are being targeted by Satan for sex trafficking, being abducted by rebels, and subjected to horrendous evil abuse. But the worst of all is that without knowing Jesus as their Savior, they will all perish in hell. It is God's people who are called to care for orphans and widows in their distress, not the government, not the humanitarian aid organizations, and not Hollywood. The church has been asleep for far too long, and it is time we wake up and get to work on this mission field! The harvest is ripe, but the workers are few!

The last decade of my life has been absolutely tumultuous. I have been to places I never dreamed of physically, emotionally, and spiritually. I mean really, I never ever wanted to go to Africa once, never mind twice. As I began this menopausal season of my life, I expected to begin the journey to a slower pace, an empty nest, and a prosperous retirement. But when I decided to be more intentional about surrendering my life to my Savior and Lord Jesus Christ, and studying the Scriptures, I got the complete opposite. I heard God telling me to do things that I couldn't imagine, and it required increased faith to choose His will and not mine. He removed the scales from my eyes, opened my ears and awakened my heart to the call of adoption. He performed amazing miracles for all to SEE that it was only God who was leading the way. My life has become more exciting than I could have ever imagined. In fact, it even turned into this book.

I believe with all my heart that God told me to write it, just like He did everything else on this journey. ***Give thanks to the LORD, call on his name; make known among the nations what he has done.*** *Sing to him, sing praise to him;* ***tell of all his wonderful acts.*** *Glory in his holy name; let the hearts of those who seek the LORD rejoice. Look to the LORD and his strength; seek his face always.* ***Remember the wonders he has done, his miracles and the judgments he pronounced*** *(Psalm 105:1-5, emphasis added).* This book was divinely inspired for the purpose of encouraging and helping others to seek God's will for themselves, and to bless them for the profit of all. God gives us everything to bless others.

If you have any encouragement from being united with Christ, if any comfort from his love, if any fellowship with the Spirit, if any tenderness and compassion, then make my joy complete by being like-minded, having the same love, being one in spirit and purpose. Do nothing out of selfish ambition or vain conceit, but in humility consider others better than yourselves. Each of you should look not only to your own interests, but also to the interests of others. Your attitude should be the same as that of Christ Jesus: Who, being in very nature God, did not consider equality with God something to be grasped, but made himself nothing, taking the very nature of a servant, being made in human likeness. And being found in appearance as a man, he humbled himself and became obedient to death—even death on a cross! Therefore God exalted him to the highest place and gave him the name that is above every name, that at the name of Jesus every knee should bow, in heaven and on earth and under the earth, and every tongue confess that Jesus Christ is Lord, to the glory of God the Father (Philippians 2:1-11).

Have you been saved by the redeeming blood of Jesus Christ? If not, won't you please ask Him to rescue you and adopt you into His family right now? Don't remain an orphan outside the family of Christ and in Satan's domain. Cry out to God, repent of your sins, humbly ask for forgiveness, and accept His sacrifice on your behalf. Then turn from your sin, and pray for the Holy Spirit to dwell in your heart and guide you to fulfill His purpose and plan for your life.

"All things have been committed to me by my Father. No one knows the Son except the Father, and no one knows the Father except the Son and those to whom the Son chooses to reveal him. Come to me, all you who are weary and burdened, and I will give you rest. Take my yoke upon you and learn from me, for I am gentle and humble in heart, and you will find rest for your souls. For my yoke is easy and my burden is light" (Matthew 11:27-30).

If you are already saved by grace, is faith the foundation of your life? Is your faith so strong that you enjoy entering God's presence? Do you study God's Word? Is there evidence of fruit in your life? *All Scripture is God-breathed and is useful for teaching, rebuking, correcting and training in righteousness, so that the man of God may be thoroughly equipped for every good work (2 Timothy 3:16).*

"Therefore everyone who hears these words of mine and puts them into practice is like a wise man who built his house on the rock" (Matthew 7:24).

Do you need to forgive? *"For if you forgive men when they sin against you, your heavenly Father will also forgive you. But if you do not forgive men their sins, your Father will not forgive your sins" (Matthew 6:14-15).*

Do you know God's plan and purpose in your life? Do you trust Him to equip you to do His will? Jesus said, *"If anyone would come after me, he must **deny himself** and **take up his cross** and **follow me**" (Matthew 16:24,* emphasis added). These three things are required to be a disciple of Jesus Christ. Denying self is painful and it means not getting our own way; but instead, choosing the will of God. This is unnatural for us as sinners; we want our own way. Taking up a cross means suffering, enduring hardship, persecution, and trials of many kinds. We tend to believe that if we are experiencing trials we are doing something wrong, but the truth is that we are probably doing something right. To follow the will of God is not easy and it will bring hard things as well as blessings. And that is okay! *Consider it pure joy, my brothers, **whenever you face trials of many kinds**, because you know that the testing of your faith develops perseverance. Perseverance must finish its work **so that you may be mature and complete, not lacking anything**. If any of you lacks wisdom, he should ask God, who gives generously to all without finding fault, and it will be given to him (James 1:2-5,* emphasis added).

Call to me and I will answer you and tell you great and unsearchable things you do not know (Jeremiah 33:3).

For the LORD gives wisdom, and from his mouth come knowledge and understanding (Proverbs 2:6).

Do you desire His will above yours? Do you hear Him speaking to you? Do you have the faith to obey Him, even when it doesn't make sense? Is God stirring your heart to adopt or get involved in orphan care? Whatever it is that God is leading you to do, don't let another minute go by without answering His call. Don't give a foothold to Satan by making excuses or procrastinating.

My prayer and purpose in writing this book is to encourage you to be strong and courageous in the Lord. Listen for His voice, get to know it, study the Scriptures, and then be about His business.

Do what He is calling you to do and get ready for a life worth living. Trust and obey, because there is no other way to be happy in Jesus. Let's all strive to live in a way that we will one day hear those words, *"Well done, my good and faithful servant."* And let's take the next generation with us into the kingdom of heaven!

For this reason I kneel before the Father, from whom his whole family in heaven and on earth derives its name. I pray that out of his glorious riches he may strengthen you with power through his Spirit in your inner being, so that Christ may dwell in your hearts through faith. And I pray that you, being rooted and established in love, may have power, together with all the saints, to grasp how wide and long and high and deep is the love of Christ, and to know this love that surpasses knowledge—that you may be filled to the measure of all the fullness of God. Now to him who is able to do immeasurably more than all we ask or imagine, according to his power that is at work within us, to him be glory in the church and in Christ Jesus throughout all generations, for ever and ever! Amen (Ephesians 3:14-21).

26 Letters From Our Family

I asked each family member to write a letter for this book. Each of us has been radically transformed and impacted; we have traveled this journey of growing our family, walking by faith, and experiencing all the trials, wonders, and miracles along the way. We have all seen the Lord clearly working in our lives. My prayer is that their letters will bless you with more insight as to how the Lord has purposed His plan in each of our lives.

JERRY'S LETTER

I was not a believer when Eileen and I met thirty-three years ago. It took ten years of struggle and heartache for me to finally surrender my life to Christ. When I accepted Christ, it was in the midst of the lowest point in our marriage, and really, in my life. It took the prospect of losing her and my daughter Melissa—our only child at the time—to drive me to my knees. Don't get me wrong, I believed in God. I was raised Roman Catholic, as Eileen was, but she developed a personal relationship with Jesus as a child. It took thirty-seven years for me to listen to the still, small voice of God calling me to Himself.

I knew there was something special about Eileen when we first met. She had the ability to connect with anyone. She had an ebullient personality that made people flock to her. People felt better when they were around her. I know that they felt better about themselves; when she wasn't encouraging them, she was making them laugh with her infectious sense of humor. This was also true for me. I felt blessed to have met her and wasted no time in making her my wife.

I should have known that the Lord was going to use her in

mighty ways. She was so full of wisdom, with the ability to perfectly articulate just what she was hearing from God. When she first started sharing what God wanted her to do, I was not very encouraging. The running response from me was: "You can't do that!" I said it so often that it almost became the title of this book.

Even though she became a Christian at an early age, it took my conversion for her to really begin to grow in her walk with the Lord. We started going to church regularly and got "plugged in" to our first church family. She watched with hopeful anticipation my response to God calling me to be a godly husband and father. I did not always do well in those areas, and they later became a point of contention in our marriage.

As Eileen grew in her walk, I noticed that her love for people grew exponentially. She had an unabashed love for Jesus that carried over into her everyday conversations. She became a strong woman of prayer and became involved in an ongoing intense study of the Bible.

I was so proud of the woman she was becoming. I was envious of her enthusiasm. I wanted what she had. I knew God wanted me to step up as a man of God, and little by little I did, but she was hearing from God and I wasn't. I became angry and disappointed in my efforts to keep up with her. It was not until I realized that we did not have to compete, and that we were on the same team, that I began hearing from God as well.

I wish my faith in Christ had been established when I was first married. Life would certainly have been less tumultuous in our early years.

One thing we always agreed on was adoption. When we first met, we each talked about how someday we would love to adopt. As the sixth of thirteen kids, I was always surrounded by kids. Not just my siblings; we always had other kids in our home. Some would just hang out for the day, and others would stay for weeks at a time. It was crazy. But our doors were always open. I guess that was how God started preparing me for a house full of kids.

It is amazing how God changes our hearts and helps us grow in certain areas. When we first started having conversations about adoption, we had no concept of how it was related to the gospel; how God commands us to care for widows and orphans. For us, at least initially, it was simply a question of adding to our family. Sure we wanted to reach out to the poor and needy, but we never really grasped the reality of God's plan until we joined Him in working to achieve it.

This is what we learned as a family. God had special plans to use us for His glory and we just needed to trust and obey. When we obeyed the voice of God, He began responding to us in miraculous ways. He answered prayer after prayer, and what was crazy was our reaction to the prayers He answered. We were blown away. What we prayed for actually came to pass and we were surprised. Why do we do this? Why do we doubt that God will answer our prayers? Is it because we don't think He is able? Or that He is too busy to concern Himself with us? One thing we have learned throughout this journey is that God does not join us when we do what we think He wants us to do, but rather He blesses us and uses us for His glory when we join Him in accomplishing His business.

This idea of joining God in working to achieve His plan was something that took some getting used to—at least for me. Years ago, I read a book called *Experiencing God*, by Henry Blackaby. What I remember most about that book was this proposition:

If you want to experience God, find out where He is at work and join Him.

What a concept! How hard could that be? I want to do that! Sure, I can do that! I trust God to provide for our daily bread. I believe He is faithful to His promises to never leave us, nor forsake us!

We learned that trusting God and believing that He is faithful turned out to be easier said than done. It was a very difficult undertaking. It took our family to some really ecstatic highs, and sunk us to some really depressing lows.

In 2004, after I had lost my job, and when money was scarce, God took us to a point where we had to depend on Him to provide like never before. It was during this time that I really grew in my faith and learned that I was not in control. Some very sweet memories were birthed during this time, and Eileen and I often look back on those days as some of the best in our married life.

It was also the time when God put an aching in our hearts for the orphans of the world. It was when I finally "got it." There are

163 million orphans in the world; 122,000 children waiting to be adopted in the United States, where there are over 320,000 churches. Why is there an orphan problem? Why are there unsaved people in the world? The same Jesus that wants us to care for the "least of these" also wants us to reach out to a lost and dying world and lead them to Him. You see, adoption is the gospel. In the same way that God can yank us out of the pit of sin and spiritual poverty and make us His child, we, through the adoption of an orphan, are able to take a child out of the pit of economic and spiritual poverty and make them our own.

J. I. Packer says that our understanding of Christianity cannot be better than our grasp of adoption. He goes on to say that if you want *to* judge how well a person understands Christianity, find out how much he makes of the thought of being God's child, and having God as his Father. It wasn't until we were well into our adoption journey that I realized this for myself.

This mission and vision of caring for orphans is God's business. We are commanded in James 1:27 to care for the widows and orphans of the world. Why? Because His heart breaks for them. Throughout the Bible, God's heart is reflected in His concern for the fatherless and the widow. When we, as believers in Christ, all begin to accept responsibility as a mission of the gospel for the orphans of the world, it will radically change how we relate to God. When we truly see the beautiful parallel between the physical adoption of an orphan and our spiritual rescue and adoption by God into His family through the atoning blood of Jesus Christ, our hearts will be knitted together with God's. Our family has been radically changed. We have drunk the Kool-Aid. There is no turning back!

Jerry

MELISSA'S LETTER

When my mom called a "family meeting" that afternoon while I was a junior in high school, I must admit, I was nervous. I always tried to get a heads-up on what could possibly be the topic of this likely loooonnnnggg affair. Most family meetings were a minimum of an hour and a half and could last up to five hours. I knew I had a lot of homework, and my mother, who believed I needed a good night's rest more than I needed an A+ average, wouldn't always let me stay up to finish it, even if it was because of a family meeting so that I couldn't complete my work before midnight. Not to mention previous family meetings included such announcements as, "We're moving!" or "We're not pleased with the spiritual fruit we see in your life. What fruit do you see?" I was on edge, to say the least.

When my mom began to tell us of her encounter with the Lord and that we were going to have "Jeremiah James" join our family, I was relieved it wasn't anything immediately life-altering, and kind of skeptical of my mother giving birth to another child. She was OLD! As the days went by, however, I felt in my soul that she was right. There was going to be another baby. I didn't know how, but I knew God had spoken.

Years later, on a Monday afternoon, while in my dorm room in Kailua-Kona, Hawaii, I would get a phone call that would change my life. "Melissa! We just got a call to pick up twin Mexican baby boys from Wilmington on Wednesday! It's Jeremiah AND James!!" The excitement was tangible. I got chills as I remembered how specific their adoption requests were, and how the social worker had told them it would never happen. I *knew* this was the Lord's doing. He gave us a preview of what was coming, and told us to have the faith that He would follow through.

I waited every day for an e-mail with photos. I called home more in those few days than I had called home in the previous year and a half of being away from home. I couldn't wait to meet these little babies. I made the decision to transfer to a school back home. I didn't want to miss out on this miracle.

I told my parents that while biological children are all a gift from God, I felt like logically you could take more credit for the conception of those kids. Adoption showed me that God had orchestrated this relationship; it seemed to me that these babies were chosen and placed with us without as much effort on our part. Sure, my parents filled out paperwork because God had led them to do so. And they prayed. But that was all they could do to prepare—until they got a phone call saying their babies were ready. It seemed so amazing to me! My faith was growing as I saw God orchestrate even minute details.

I remember first meeting them and being hesitant to love them. They were so small and connected to so many machines. It felt risky to get attached to them, but despite my best efforts, I fell head over heels fairly quickly. I did the night shift in rotation with my parents; I sang to them, I cuddled them, I changed their diapers. I called them "*My* boys."

My sister was in her glory having little baby brothers, and she was adamant even early on that my parents should adopt again. Some kids talked about music nonstop, or maybe their favorite activity, but Ellie talked about adoption. I didn't know if anything would ever come of her passion, with how much work the boys had been with all their health issues, and how my dad had been out of work, and how old my parents were getting. My parents stepped out in faith for a China adoption, and then the wait began. I still didn't know how things would pan out. I thought Ellie would get involved in adoption on her own. Or I would adopt. Because despite it being something I'd always thought of as a great thing, once my family adopted, it sparked within me a passion for the orphan that I didn't have before. I encouraged others to think beyond adoption as "Plan B," which is only if they couldn't have biological children, and urged them to pray about adoption as a "Plan A." Years later, when I met my husband, Randy, I asked him his thoughts on adoption. I knew if he was against it, I could never marry him, but thankfully he was, and is, open to the idea and we hope to pursue adoption in our future.

One day in February 2007, my mom called Randy and me over for a family meeting, and I had that same nervous feeling. I called other family members to see if I could get a heads-up on the topic. Nobody helped me out. We arrived to discover that the Lord had spoken again, and that despite the fact they had aged out of China, they were still going to adopt again: this time from Ethiopia. We watched videos and read all the information. This adoption could be finalized this same year! And we even had names again!

I knew better than to question this. Not only because of my mom's encounter with the Word, but because even as she said it,

I felt it was true. I can't explain it, but I knew deep down that we were on board to witness another miracle. Within a week they had $25,000 coming to them and my faith was strengthened. When they got their referral, and the twins and a sibling matched my family's requests, I knew other people were seeing God at work as well. Another miraculous God-ordained relationship.

Being a photographer, I wanted to go with them to Ethiopia to take photos of this adventure, but in July I found out I was pregnant and was therefore unable to get all the required vaccines. Instead, Randy and I would be able to care for the boys while both parents and Ellie went to Ethiopia. We were so thrilled to meet these babies and I cried like a baby at the airport when we picked them up. My faith was strengthened once more as I saw other people answer the call God had placed on their lives by watching my family step forward in faith.

As a small child I used to pray every day for a sibling. And twins. I did not like being an only child. I was seven years old before my brother was born. I was ecstatic when I got a baby sister three years later. God answered my prayer. Little did I know that He had more in store for us. I am now the oldest of *eight* siblings. Five of which are closer in age to my own kids, but hey, they're still my siblings. I like to think God answered my prayer for twins with the boys, and then Ellie's prayer for twins with the girls. And Josiah is a treasure that we all prayed for. We are so blessed to be a part of these miracles.

I am so grateful to be a part of a family who chooses to trust and obey, even when it doesn't make sense, even when the going gets tough ... because they are showing the world, and us, their kids, what it means to follow Christ wherever He leads, at whatever cost, and know that He will provide.

Melissa

RANDY'S LETTER

My first contact with the Mestas family came through a

burgeoning relationship with their oldest daughter, Melissa. Our relationship did not grow in a vacuum, as the Mestas clan sticks close together. Much of our time "getting to know each other" happened in a family setting over dinner and up very late in deep conversations with her parents. Melissa and I did not do the "typical" dating routine which usually goes like: hanging out on weekends, going to movies, and talk about life when we can be distracted by anything else at the moment. Rather, we had a very intentional relationship that grew under the supervision of a loving family who wanted to ensure their daughter was cared for and treated respectfully. Heck, Eileen even had ninety-five questions in her arsenal to promote lively discussions. This family was definitely the closest contact I had with an adoptive family; I became an adopted member myself when I married Melissa. At this time they just had Jeremiah and James. I learned about how they came to get them and saw firsthand what an integral part of the family they had become in just two years.

I feel that I am very privileged to see an adoptive family from the inside out. I probably always wondered how these situations really worked out, and if the families or the children loved one another in the same way as normal families; but I never thought about it seriously until now. I was surprised when Eileen and Jerry told us that they were going to adopt again. I mean they had the twins and still had a lot going on with their biological kids as well. I knew them well enough to know that they would not make such a decision lightly. I had heard about God's provision for the first adoption, and now I was going to experience the adoption process from God's prompting all the way through its fruition. Watching the Mestas family walk out their faith in God's desire for them to adopt from Ethiopia taught me about the depths of God's love and provision. God taught me about how His love for us should spur us on to extend that love to those that have long been forgotten by the church. Adoption, as I have learned, is a perfect picture of God's love applied to this broken world. What better way to show people that our God is love, than to reach out into the world and pluck someone out of an impossibly hopeless existence? In the instance of Keren, Keziah, and Josiah, God saw fit to impress upon this family to step out in faith, knowing they had neither the resources nor capability to rescue these little ones.

My questions about the assimilation of adopted children into their families were answered quite quickly after the final trip to bring the newest Mestas children home. There was no sense that they were going to pick up some other people's kids, bring them home, and hope it worked out to where they could love them. Rather, just like our Father does, they loved them before they knew one another. It was really amazing to see a family committed to following the leading of our God in a way that would send three family members to Africa and see them return as six. Yes, these children looked different than the majority of the family, but they were no less a part of it. The act of adoption was one of joyful obedience for this family. As many Christians know, obedience to God does not come without its trials, but these too were met with the understanding that God was writing this story, and He would receive glory from even the trials. I could tell that these new little ones were as Mestas to the family as my wife is, and I knew this firsthand, because I loved them the same too.

But wait, there's more! Really, guys, what else is there for you to do? Shortly after Jerry and Eileen catch their breath from adopting Keren, Keziah, and Josiah, they keep talking about this boy they met in Kolfe when they were in Ethiopia. They felt God leading them to support Solomon until they could figure out a possible adoption solution. He ended up being too old to legally adopt, but was able to come live with them and study at a local college. I saw this family rally around Solomon and pour into him every ounce of love they could. God saw fit to have Solomon separate from the Mestas family, but not before a great awareness was raised about the poor conditions in the Kolfe Orphanage and over $50,000 was raised. The journey with Solomon was difficult to watch break down. It did, however, teach me that God can teach us through both times of great joy and great sadness.

My experiences with the Mestas family and their adoption journeys have encouraged me to consider whether or not I would like to one day adopt. My wife and I have been blessed with three biological children, but we do sense that God would have us adopt in the future. I love the example of God's love that an adoptive family presents to the world, especially if more than one race is represented. People cannot help but ask, what is going on there? Something is different. We are not currently pursuing an adoption, but in the meantime we feel that it is important that we support others in their adoption journeys. As God blesses us, we hope to pass on that blessing in any way we can, be that through prayer, spiritual encouragement or financially. It is my hope that as you come to understand the Mestases' journey, you too are inspired to ask yourself what role God would have you play in the world of adoption and orphan care. Orphans number in the multimillions, yet "Christians" far exceed that mark. It is time that we awake from our comfortable slumber and ask our God to use us mightily to rescue His little ones.

Randy

JONATHAN'S LETTER

I really don't even know where to start ... Every day is another adventure in the Mestas' house. Some good days, some bad days, never any boring days!

Growing up, I had heard about adoption and my best friend was even adopted. But I didn't see a lot of adoptions happening. I liked the idea and knew that there were many kids out there in the world who needed families. However, when my parents finally started to break down to my little sister, Ellie's, constant barrage of adoption requests, I was a bit skeptical. I thought it would be different to have adopted siblings. I thought that every time you looked at that child you would think, "You aren't really my brother/ sister ..." "You don't really belong here ..." I just couldn't wrap my head around it for the first few initial weeks of researching adoption. But, the more we looked into it and prayed about it, the more open I became to it.

In fact, by the time we found out we had thirty-six hours to pick up Jeremiah and James, I was literally freaking out, and so excited to finally have some brothers. When my mom got that phone call, I screamed, jumped on the couch, flew over the couch, and slammed my head on the coffee table. I quickly recovered and continued rejoicing ecstatically! I absolutely fell in love with them as I realized they are my real brothers intentionally delivered by God. They just came a different way!

Round two of our adoption journey was way easier to process. I knew that if God wanted my family to adopt again, then it would happen, no matter what! If He said to do it, then you better do it; yes, sir, no questions asked. Well, that was my perspective anyway. My parents had quite a few questions, but they still obeyed the call.

Each adoption journey has had its mountaintop and valley experiences, but we have learned together that there is nothing too big for God to handle. Looking back now at my initial feelings about adoption and at how our family has grown in faith and knowledge of the Lord, I realize my initial concerns and thoughts were false; they were lies and a distraction from the enemy.

When I take all the 'littles' out shopping with me, sometimes I get the strangest looks from people. I still don't understand why that is. … Ha ha! Some people have asked me if it's weird to have siblings of a different color, and I always find it interesting that it even matters to people. I don't notice that they don't look like me. I don't love them any less than my two biological sisters. It's hard to explain the love that connects adoptive families to those who don't understand how God adopts us into His family. Sometimes I feel like it's the same as talking to a brick. So, I would rather just try to live my life to show them.

I have learned a lot through this last ten-year journey that my family has been on. I've learned about the power of prayer, the strength that a little faith can give, the power of God's Word, and just how blessed I am to have been placed in the middle of His awesome plan. Like I said, "It isn't always easy living in the Mestas' house, but it is definitely never boring!"

Jonathan

SOLOMON'S LETTER

I met the Mestas family in 2007 for the first time. I remember I was studying for the upcoming final exam when I saw many kids run to Eileen and they gave her a warm greeting. Then I said to myself, I had to talk to that woman and I did. The Mestas family was on a tour of the Kolfe Orphanage and I joined them. We were talking for more than an hour that day. Finally, Eileen told all the Kolfe boys to make a line and then she started giving them hugs and kisses. This was the first time something like that happened in the Kolfe Orphanage. She gave me a big hug as well and then they left. From that moment I knew that God brought this family into my life for a reason.

To our surprise, they came back to Kolfe again the next day. They brought soccer balls for the kids and everyone was happy to see them again. We all had a great time talking to them. This time they spent more than two hours with us until it was time to say good-bye again. Everyone was sad when they realized that it was time for them to go back to America. Before they left Kolfe, Eileen gave her e-mail address to one of the boys and said we could write to her. I had no idea how to use a computer at that time, but I didn't ask for her home address.

One week later, I asked my friend to make me an e-mail address and teach me how to send e-mail messages. My friend got me a new e-mail address with two pages of instructions that show how to use e-mail step by step. Then I sent my first e-mail, which was a request to call the Mestas family as my family. Then they told me I can call them my family.

Since then we have been talking via e-mail and Skype even till today. They tried to adopt me, but I was too old for adoption. That was heart-breaking for both of us. But we knew that God has stored something better for us. We kept praying for one another until the miraculous day came when God brought me to America two years later.

I told them I wanted to study computers and they were looking for a computer school here in Ethiopia. Instead, God created an opportunity for me to go to Southeastern College in America. To be honest, I hadn't any desire to go to this school because they did not teach computers. I was shocked when I heard this news. I prayed to God to show me if He really wanted me to do this. Then finally, I decided to attend this college. I got here June 23, 2010, in

Raleigh, North Carolina. There were around 100 people gathered at the airport to congratulate me and I was interviewed by ABC News. It was an awesome experience.

After a few months, I had some difficulties adjusting to everything and going to this school. I thought it was better for me to go back to Ethiopia, but then God allowed another opportunity for me to continue to study in America. Now I live in New York and I am studying my favorite course, computer technology. This was something I was praying for a long time. Finally I got it. God's timing is perfect. I am so grateful for what God did in my life through the Mestas family and I love and miss them all. But we all know that God has a plan for me and I look forward to what He has in store for my future.

I love and miss you all,

Solomon

ELLIE'S LETTER

At the beginning of this journey, I was a little girl whose ears had heard of the Lord. Nearly ten years later, these eyes of mine have seen the Lord. I have seen Him answer prayers and work in ways that I could have never even thought to pray for. I have felt His goodness and His grace so closely in both the good times and the hard times; and I am fully convinced that my God is a faithful God, despite my faithlessness.

God had put it on my heart to pray for a baby brother or sister (preferably both and in the form of twins) constantly since I was about three years old. I remember carrying my own diaper bag so people would think it was my baby brother or sister's. I often cried myself to sleep begging God to bring a baby to my family, and I would even ride my bike around my neighborhood, hoping to find an abandoned baby in the bushes (or a puppy, but a baby was my first choice). I don't know whether it was the fact that my dearest childhood friend was adopted, or if it had something to do with all the hours spent reenacting *Anne of Green Gables* and playing orphanage with my baby dolls … all I know is that God sang His song for orphans to my heart and it is a song that is meant to be sung loud and clear.

When my parents felt God leading them to adopt a baby boy domestically, I was nine years old. I was ecstatic and began cranking up the twin prayers, begging God to allow us to have two babies that needed a family, instead of just one. (Plus, I didn't want to have to fight my other siblings over who got to hold the baby. You know? Logistics and such.) I can still see that moment frozen in time when my dad came bounding up the stairs to announce that we had gotten a call for twin baby boys. I remember the screams ringing throughout the house and my brother dripping water all over, as he left the shower in a frenzy. I remember my mom replaying the voicemail message from the caseworker, and I remember the note on the counter for the next two days amidst the lists of things to do: "Must pick them up by Wednesday at 2:30 if you want them."

Most importantly, I remember the awe that settled over my heart as I realized: God had answered my prayers and He had brought us twins. We knew they were sick, but after seeing God work so mightily, we were ready to trust Him again. There was no room for doubt that these were the ones. Jeremiah **and** James.

However, after a few weeks of machines (that sound similar to the screeching eels in *The Princess Bride*) beeping every two seconds because of a loose strap on a baby's chest, it started to get old for me. **Really old.** You see, when I prayed all those years for a baby brother or sister, I meant the kind that you could hold without having to remain within three feet of the wires that they were strapped to. I meant the kind that I could play with and not have to wonder if they would ever be able to sit up and see me playing peek-a-boo with them. I thought that God had chosen a pretty rude way to answer a kid's prayer. Here I was thinking He had heard me, when He actually sent me two baby invalids. That was when He spoke to me about true adoption.

You were helpless to save yourself and I took you in. You had nothing exciting to offer Me, but I loved you anyway. You had no hope of survival, but then I cared for you.

You were an orphan that was outside of My family, oblivious to your need for Me. Now you are My child.

Love these babies the way that I love you. With agape love. A love that is not self-seeking. A love that hopes. A love that perseveres (1 Corinthians 13:4-13).

God gave me such a deep love for them through this revelation that I wouldn't have taken all the healthy babies in the world for my two scrawny baby brothers! They may have been sick and at risk of never being able to talk or play tag or ride a bike, but they were handpicked for my family and hand-delivered by a mighty God who never makes mistakes. Loving them didn't depend on whether or not they could play with me some day. I need only love them because they were created by God and given to me to love. **This was the beginning of what God is doing in my heart. He showed me who I was and who He is through two sickly baby boys.**

When you have been loved with this agape love, it changes you. It needs to be shared and given as freely as it is received. I knew my family was to adopt again. There were too many kids in the world just like my baby brothers; children who needed the love and protection of a family. There were too many kids in the world just like me, an orphan in need of the healing love of Jesus.

After nearly one thousand days of reading articles aloud and showing videos and sharing adoption program information and agency websites and waiting child lists and MUCH praying for God to PLEASE AWAKEN MY PARENTS TO THE LIGHT(!!!), He did just that. In His perfect timing and in His perfect way, He awakened my parents' hearts to His plan for a precious little boy whose Mama was sick, and his two little sisters who were being born on the other side of the world.

In the beginning, I was just asking for one sister from China. Thankfully, God's vision was for something much bigger. He wanted to bring three more children into our family and do it in a way that would inspire others to go out and love the children we could not bring home.

Through Jeremiah and James' adoption, God revealed His heart for the orphan and true adoption to me. Through the adoption of Keziah, Keren and Josiah, and traveling to Ethiopia, God opened my eyes to a much bigger picture of His heart for the world. When

I went to Ethiopia, I met orphans the same age as me, the only difference between us being the fact that their parents were dead and mine were still alive, and it broke my heart. When I came home I knew that God had much more for me to do than I would have ever dreamed. Within the next few years, He had me advocating for His children in ways that I had never anticipated. He led me to speak at churches and conferences and youth groups on behalf of God's heart for the orphan and our response as Christians to His heart for them; regardless of our age. God also took me to serve in orphanages in Guatemala, China, and Uganda. Today, I am enrolled in Nursing School with the goal to become a midwife, so that I can help prevent children from becoming orphans in the first place.

This journey God has placed on my family has certainly shaped the exterior of my life; I went from being the baby of three children to the third of eight children, within four years. In elementary and middle school, I learned to love and care for sick babies. I learned to resuscitate little boys who would forget to breathe when they drank their bottles, and I learned to accept bodily fluids as a major part of life. I learned to work apnea monitors and heart monitors and help around the house in ways I wouldn't have if everyone wasn't so busy caring for the boys. I spent the majority of my high school years toting around my sweet African babies, teaching myself how to be diligent in school, and planning the next mission trip to love the babies who didn't yet have families. This wasn't what I had foreseen, even in my best dreams. It was tremendously hard and not nearly as glamorous as it sounds, yet it was glorious.

However, all the external changes aside, the real shaping God has done on this journey has been in my heart. If my parents had not stepped out in faith and obedience, I would not know Jesus the way that I do today. I would not have seen God's faithfulness in the ways that I have, and I would not know the joy that comes from trusting Jesus with my whole heart. (Not to mention, I would be horribly selfish and incapable of multi-tasking.) Worst of all, I wouldn't know the five biggest blessings to my heart and life. My 'littles': Jeremiah, James, Josiah, Keziah, and Keren are my treasures here on earth and I am the most blessed sister on the earth below and in the heavens above.

Papa and Mama, I thank you so very much for not writing me

off as just some little kid who was obsessed with orphans. Thank you for listening for the still, small voice of the Lord and being such a beautiful example of lives surrendered to His will. You inspire me to continue listening for His voice and being obedient to His bidding.

To the reader, I pray that this story will grow your heart as much as it has mine. May it draw you closer to the God who gives us life and may it inspire you to be a vessel of His love to the children who He has created with such great purpose. He demonstrated His love for us in this: that while we were yet sinners—His enemies—He sent His Son, Jesus, to die for us in our place and rise again on the third day; conquering our sin and the death that came with it, eternally securing our future as His adopted children. That love is unlike anything the world has ever known and is surely enough cause for obedience. If God has taught me anything on this journey, He's taught me that those we are called to love don't have to be lovely, and most of the time, they won't be. I most definitely wasn't lovely when He came for me. Yet by His grace, from one redeemed orphan to another, we can let the love of Jesus take root in our hearts and let it heal us together. In His love, by His love, through His love, we will be made lovely.

Ellie

JEREMIAH'S LETTER

I am nine years old and one minute older than my twin brother, James. It is nice to be adopted and I hope more people will adopt more kids. Sometimes it is crazy being in a big family. There is always a lot of noise and it's crazy sometimes. I like to go downstairs to my grandma's house where it is quieter. I like to visit my grandma and we talk a lot.

It is a miracle that I was adopted. A miracle means God did something special to make us a family. God wanted us to be a family. I know God cares about me and never leaves me.

I think it is good that our family is different colors because God gave us to each other. Sometimes I get embarrassed when people stare at us and when I see other families all one color. But I love my family.

I like to hear about my birth family and I really want to see them some day. I am happy that I have everybody that loves me. I have fun and I feel safe.

It is good to be homeschooled. I like to be in my house with my mama, papa, brothers and sisters, and my grandma and our two dogs, Ruby and Sammy. My favorite subject is reading and making fun things. I like to learn about God and science. I like to go outside and learn about bugs, birds, fish, and all of creation. I like swimming and baseball and going fishing and camping too.

I was really happy when Solomon came home to live with us, but now I am very sad that he left. I am really happy that we are writing this book and I hope that it will help more kids to be adopted. I want there to be no more orphans and that more people will know God.

Love, Jeremiah

JAMES'S LETTER

I am nine years old and a twin. I like Legos and schoolwork. I have been growing in a crazy family because we are busy all day. It got even busier now with this book Mom is writing, and it has been a hard year for us with everything that happened.

I try to be good and help my mom and make sure everything goes well while she is at the cottage writing our book. I love to cook with my mom and I have been cooking a lot for my family and doing chores. I cook breakfast and lunch. If I smell something burning, I turn off the stove. I love to cook for my brothers and sisters, but it is hard when they don't want the same thing. I can barely handle it; it is more than I can handle, but sometimes I just have to do it. It's not very easy, but I try. I make sure the kids are quiet and good so Papa can do his work too. Ellie takes good care of us, but I help her. I also like to eat dinner with my grandma downstairs in her house. My grandpa died three years ago and I don't like my grandma to be alone. I pray every day that my grandma will become a Christian.

Homeschooling is fun. I am working hard at reading. I like to read in my bed with my book light. Since I learned to read, now I can read this book by myself. I like science and exercising. I like swimming, baseball, and our co-op class. I like to go to Bible study and Awana. We build lots of stuff with our Legos and we want to be in the *LEGO Club* magazine. We also love to build things at the Home Depot and Lowe's workshop classes for kids.

I think being in a family of different colors is like the rainbow. We wear the same color clothes so we don't get lost when we go out. It is easier for Mom to keep track of us. But at home, we wear different colored clothes. I don't care about being a family of different colors. I only get embarrassed when the kids don't behave.

My favorite food is Mexican and Jeremiah's favorite is taco soup.

This book is being written because God told us to and if we don't obey Him, we will be disciplined. I think this book will help people to adopt other children. It doesn't matter if they are white, brown or maybe different colors. It doesn't matter to God because God made everyone different, and He loves us all.

A miracle is something God has in mind, but it may be hard to understand. But it will turn out all right. God gave me a miracle from when I had a brain bleed when I was born. A miracle from God happened and He healed me. My birth parents couldn't take care of me, but God gave me a new family. I'm glad that I have a good family. I miss my birth family, but I am not mad. I hope they become Christians too. I am glad I am a Christian or else I wouldn't be blessed with the salvation that God gave me. I gave my heart to Jesus and I love Him. I am glad I was adopted and I will continue being glad and praise God for being adopted.

I hope you will enjoy this book my mom wrote and you laugh, cry, and trust God in your life. Maybe adopt a child and help Show Hope with sending money to them, which will help a child get adopted. If you don't adopt, you can still help a child. Please help them. You can sponsor a child or write them letters. It sounds like a silly thing, but you will have a good time helping kids. It will be a good time to teach them about the Bible and your life will turn out better. Sometimes Satan attacks the teenagers when they get big, so it is good to teach them the Bible too. We have a story about

Solomon in this book when he didn't want to learn about the Bible. He wanted to learn about computers. You might go through some hard times when you adopt kids and if you did, this book might help you change your life. With the Bible you can have a good time teaching the gospel to the kids in a different country.

It feels good to be a big brother and help teach my siblings. I try to be nice, but sometimes I just can't, because sometimes they will not do what I tell them. It is not easy!

It was hard when we adopted my brother and sisters from Ethiopia. Josiah didn't speak English, so we didn't know what he was saying until we heard him sing the alphabet. That was his first song in English. My baby sisters were so tiny and it was funny to play with their cheeks. When they were four years old they were laughing when I told them I liked to do that to them. I want to adopt children when I grow up.

What has God taught you so far? I hope you will believe this book. I know it is not the Bible, but my mom put the Bible verses that are true in it. I am glad that we are adopted and I hope you will get adopted by Jesus Christ as your Savior too.

Love, James

JOSIAH'S LETTER

I was three years old when I was adopted. I remember my birth mom holding Keziah and Keren in her hands and I was looking at them. There was no clean water and we ate injera and I didn't like it. It was terrible when I slept on the floor at my house in Ethiopia. I am sad that my birth dad died. I am sad I had to be adopted because I left my best mom. I am happy that she became a Christian.

When God said I am getting a new Mom and Dad I was happy, but I thought they were going to be brown, because I never saw white people. I was scared at the foster house with all the big kids who were mean to me. I saw a white lady come with her purse and she took one of the big boys, and I got scared that she was going to take me. I was scared and crying when my family came to get me. Then I sat on their lap and they gave me a granola bar and I stopped crying.

When we got to the hotel, I got coloring books and cars with a track and I had fun. I went in the bathtub for the first time and didn't want to get out. I wanted to stay in there and I loved swimming in the pool at the hotel too.

I love my birth mom, but it was not very fun in Ethiopia all alone. I am happy I was adopted with my baby sisters. But I don't like twins on this side of me and two on the other side of me, because they both boss me around.

It is a miracle that I got adopted and got home safely and that no one else took me before my mom and dad, because we are the lucky ones. God cares about me. He gives us water and food and my family. I want a little brother now.

Having a family with different colors is half good and half sad. Mostly everyone in my family is white. White people scared me before and I never saw a woman with glasses. It is bad that I am the only brown boy in my family. I wish we were all brown, but not my grandma and grandpa. I want another brown brother like me.

Homeschooling is fun. I like to be home with my family and play. I like math and my favorite sports are baseball and swimming. I love to go to the beach and drink salty water and ride on the waves with my boogie board.

I am happy we are writing this book to change everyone's and our lives. If they read it, it might help them adopt other kids that are on the streets. I wish everyone in America could adopt all the kids in Ethiopia, so that they won't be hurt anymore and die. I am adopted two times because Jesus adopted me and my family did too! Amen!

Love, Josiah

KEZIAH'S LETTER

I am five years old and I am in kindergarten. I am learning to write and read. I like to play with my dolls, ride my bike and swim. I was nine months old when I came home to be with my forever family. When the nanny at the Gladney Foster House handed me to my new family, I started to scream and cry so loud that they had to take me away from them for a little while. I had never seen white people before and they scared me. After a little while, they gave me to my mom and dad again, and I have been happy ever since then. If we didn't get adopted, we would live in the orphanage and we could die. I am happy I was adopted with my brother too. We would have never lived together in the orphanage. We got healthy and we got food and we love all of our family. I love and miss my birth mom and I want to go visit Ethiopia someday. I know Jesus loves me and I pray He takes care of everybody in the world. Please help other children get adopted.

Love, Keziah

KEREN'S LETTER

I am five years old and I am in kindergarten. I love to write and I am learning to read and spell. I love to ride my bike, swim, draw, and color pictures. I was born one hour after my sister Kezzie. When the nanny at the Gladney Foster Home handed me to my new family, I was smiling and so happy to see them. They told me I never cried for three days, when they were in Ethiopia. I am the happy and funny jokester in the house. I like to make people laugh. I also sing all the time and Mama tells me I have a gift of singing. I just can't stop singing, even in my sleep! I am so happy that I was adopted because everyone in my family loves me. Jesus loves me. I love my mom and dad and brothers and sisters and all of my family and friends. Please help more children get adopted and love them all day long.

Love, Keren

GRANDMA'S LETTER

When Jerry and Eileen adopted the twin boys, we were very happy for them and us! We all enjoyed seeing them thrive and grow into two healthy, precious boys. God knows they got all the love and care we could all give them. They were such a joy to all of us, and Eileen and Ellie, especially, worked so hard taking care of their needs and still do. As the boys got stronger, healthier, and older, they didn't need as much care. Life seemed to be getting a little easier around the house ... "HA HA!" Then they told us they were going to adopt THREE CHILDREN FROM ETHIOPIA! They said it was going to specifically be nine-month-old twin girls and their three-year-old brother.

Well, the entire family thought they had lost their minds! They were not getting any younger and they were far from wealthy. Jerry had lost his job and it took quite a while to find another one, almost three years! Money was always tight, to say the least, so they said they were going to start this adoption journey on faith!

Well, I have to admit, I have witnessed one miracle in this house after another. It's hard to believe it all, especially if you didn't see it with your own eyes. When the children arrived, they brought so much more joy with them into our family. But now it was even more work with five 'littles.' It was a big adjustment for all of us, but especially for the children. But with lots of love and care, it took some time, and everything seemed to be normal again. "Whatever that is?" Money is still always tight and it's always a lot of craziness and a lot of work, but I could not imagine our lives without them. We love them all so very much and they love us right back. I am very proud of their decision to adopt all these children. Somehow, they seem to manage and keep it all going. And the miracles are still coming, giving them the strength and love to do whatever needs to be done.

Jerry is a great father and he works very hard too. God gives His blessings in this home every single day.

My husband and I are so proud of Eileen and always have been. Our whole family, her sisters, brother, aunts, uncles, and cousins are all so very proud, but we all still think they are a little crazy. To take all of this responsibility on at their age is just crazy. But we have all come to admire their dedication and the love they give to all eight of their children and three grandchildren and all of their family and friends too. "THIS IS DEFINITELY A GOD THING!"

With all our love always,

Mom and Dad

27 Acknowledgments

It is with sincere humility and gratitude that I give thanks, first and foremost, to the Creator God and Lord Jesus Christ for rescuing me from being an orphan in this world and destined for an eternity in hell. He opened my eyes, ears, and heart to receive His call to accept His loving sacrifice that paid the debt for my sins. I am so grateful to be adopted into the family of God, with all my sins, past, present and future having been forgiven and washed away white as snow. I now have a future and a hope of eternal life in heaven with Him and all the saints. He has blessed me with a loving and wonderful family who I love with all of my heart. He has entrusted eight beautiful children to my care and is faithful to carry and equip me in all things. He is my shepherd, my rock, and my hope. I am eternally grateful for all the blessings and trials that continue to keep me on my knees and at the throne of grace.

To my husband, Jerry, who has been living this amazing journey with me for thirty-three years and supporting me in everything the Lord has purposed. Although your initial response was usually "You can't do that!"—you prayed, sought counsel and wisdom, and eventually surrendered to the will of God for our lives. Thank you for growing together with me in the knowledge of Jesus Christ and for working so hard to provide, protect, and lead our family on this journey. Thank you for encouraging and supporting me to follow God's call on my life, to be a stay-at-home mom, an inventor, patent and business owner, homeschool mom, in ministry, and to write this book. Thank you for being such a wonderful husband, father, son-in-law, father-in-law, and Grandpa. I am grateful for the way you love and support me and our family and for always being the comic relief! Thank you for making our home a safe, loving and happy place where the Lord Jesus Christ and Holy Spirit dwell! You truly are a gift from God to us all.

To my Sweet Ellie (Ellie Marie, cute as can be!), who is responsible for so much of this testimony becoming a reality. The Lord clearly used you as a young child to speak to our hearts that HE had a plan for us to grow our family through adoption. Thank you for being my right hand in caring for the 'littles,' and being a second Mama to them. I know this was not an easy task, especially while juggling your responsibilities with school and ministry. Thank you for your faith, love, compassion, obedience, love for the Lord Jesus and His Holy Word, and your servant's heart. I could not have done any of this without you. You are truly an inspiration and a living example of 1 Timothy 4:12: *Don't let anyone look down on you because you are young, but set an example for the believers in speech, in life, in love, in faith and in purity.* You are a shining light in this world! *"Let your light shine before men, that they may see your good deeds and praise your Father in heaven" (Matthew 5:16).* Thank you for being a wonderful daughter, sister, granddaughter, and auntie! Thank you for being instrumental in the adoption of more than 100 precious children, in addition to serving so many others in orphanages in China, Guatemala, Ethiopia, and Uganda. You are a true blessing and inspiration to us all!

To Melissa, Randy and Jonathan, I thank you from the bottom of my heart for all of your love, support, and dedicated service that also enabled us to walk this journey by faith. I could not have done any of this without you stepping in to care for the 'littles,' pray, and serve us all so well when we really needed you. I know it was not easy on any of you, especially since you were all going to school, working on your careers, starting your own family, and juggling our crazy lives along with yours. Thank you for supporting your mama even when you thought it was crazy to do so, and always being there no matter what. I am forever grateful and thank my God for each of you!

To my mom and dad, Babe and Betty Farrell: Thank you for being such wonderful examples of dedicated, loving parents and grandparents. Thank you for supporting us in all of this craziness, even when you thought none of it made any sense. Thank you for loving all of us so well, cooking all the meals, and faithfully being here with us every time we needed you. Thank you for being the best parents and grandparents a child could dream of! Thank you for loving Jerry like your own son and supporting us in every way possible for thirty-three years! You have been our greatest support team and played a major role in our marriage restoration. Look what we would have missed if we had divorced twenty-two years ago. I thank my God for you and all the blessings you have bestowed upon us! I am grateful for all the family HE has given me!

To my sweet 'sistah' and homeschool mentor, Beth Herbert: You have been my right arm in my homeschooling journey and a loyal and faithful friend. You have been the ear, sounding board, and journal keeper of my crazy life for fifteen years. For many years I told you I felt the Lord was telling me to write this book and I needed you to help me remember everything. Thank you for always being my cheerleader, encouraging and supporting me, and being my co-editor in writing this book. I could not have done this without you. I could not have homeschooled without you to guide, encourage, and keep me informed of all the events our children have attended together over the years. We have so many wonderful memories. Thank you for starting our local homeschool support group, and blessing hundreds of families with your loving and dedicated service with your passion for homeschooling. Thank you for always speaking truth of the Word of God and pointing me to Him throughout the years, keeping me focused on the calling! You are truly a treasure and gift in my life.

Thank you to Solomon, for having the desire and courage to write me a letter asking me to be your mama. You changed my life forever. You took me deep into the heart of orphanage life, places of pain, suffering and despair, and taught me agape love. You opened places in my heart that I didn't know existed and gave me a deeper understanding of the heart of God. I am proud of how hard you worked to become the valedictorian that changed the course of your life. I am grateful the Lord brought you to America to be a part of our family and tHIS story. I pray as you continue your journey of seeking God's will for your life, you will strive to bring honor and glory to Him. I will always love you forever, for always, no matter what!

To the birth parents of our five beautiful adopted babies: Thank you for CHOOSING LIFE! Thank you for having the courage to go to the adoption agency to find another family for "our" babies, when you knew you could not handle this responsibility. Thank you for walking through your pain and suffering with sacrificial love and compassion for these babies. Thank you for the hope that God had another plan for their lives and for thinking of their future more than your own convenience. It took much sacrifice, conviction, and courage to make this choice ... one that I regretfully did not make when I was in your same situation as a young woman. I know you all suffered much pain and anguish in making this decision. I am forever grateful! I love you for giving me the opportunity to be the Mama to love, cherish, and raise these beautiful children in the admonition of the Lord. It is an honor and privilege to teach them about you, pray for you, and share how much you mean to us, because of your decision to trust us with their lives. I thank my God for each of you who played a role in making us a family! God is the master of turning ashes into beauty!

To Jeremiah, James, Josiah, Keziah, and Keren: You are all our precious, divinely and miraculously appointed children that we love with all of our hearts. I thank my God for creating each one of you and intentionally placing you in my life. It is my honor and privilege to be your mama and your teacher. Of all the millions of women in the world, He chose me to be the most blessed ... to be YOUR MAMA! You are my joy and my reason for living. You have all taught me how to love deeper, hurt harder, to die more to myself, and have more compassion. You have taken me to new depths of understanding the heart of God. I am in awe that He saw fit to bless my life with each one of you. While I know I am never going to be perfect, and I will make lots of mistakes; I pray I will serve, teach, and guide you to love the Lord with all of your heart, soul, mind, and strength. There is nothing more important to do with the rest of my life than to love and care for you. I am blessed more than I deserve!

I am forever grateful to all of my family, friends and saints in the church, who played a vital role in tHIS journey. Thank you for all the prayers and support through all the trials and triumphs, especially during our season of unemployment, adoptions, and Kolfe Orphanage Ministry. We could not have done any of this without you all. We have been truly blessed by the body of Christ functioning by the Word of God. I pray the Lord's richest blessings upon each and every one of you, who allowed the Lord to use you for HIS purpose and for HIS glory. We are eternally grateful!

Thank you to Children's Home Society of North Carolina—Brenda Farnsworth; The Gladney Center for Adoption—Debra Parris, Mary Thottukadavil, Scott Brown, Ryan & Abby Brown, Belay, Tafesse; Show Hope—Steven Curtis & Mary Beth Chapman, Scott Hasenbalg, Dan & Terri Coley, Wendy Cosby, Kathy McKinney, and all Show Hope supporters; Sarah Gesiriech and the team of the President George W. Bush Administration who created the Adoption Tax Credit; Scott & Theresa Haven; Don & Cathi Albright; Jim & Becky Sherrer; Tom & Kim Brown; Michael & Mary Haley; Jeff & Myra Smyth; The Talbott Family; Ruth Talbott; Matthew & Joanne Page; Mike & Sue Thorpe; Bethany Pease Sheets; The Pease Family; Ron & Paula; Rebecca, Sam, John Paul, Abigail Taylor; Jeffery & Glenda Howard; Alex & Pat Mestas; Gaby Mestas & Dave Thoits; Jay & Dena Hughes; Derwin, Faye & Emma Creech; Jim & Maria Hall; Jaclyn Bermudez; Bob & Carla Craig; Chuck & Cyndee Farrell; Jack & Debi Argila; Linda & Gary DeFriest; Lauren & Ben Forney; Corrie Daming & Daming Family; Carlos & Colleen Mestas; Lloyd & Melissa Mestas; Becky Mestas; Louis & Carol Mestas; Todd & Clellie Allen; Janet Rose Allen; the *Wake Weekly* newspaper; Ned & Brett Winn; David & Amy Smelley; Timmy & Miranda Vatterott; Michael & Mary Moore; Marvin & Bonnie Moore; Dorothy McAteer; Mickey Boccio; Patricia Burke; Mike & Teresa George; Deanna & Mark Falchook; Scott & Debra Brown; Jason & Janet Dohm; Chris & Tracey Rafferty; Jodi Jackson Tucker; Kiel & Carolyn Twietmeyer; Melanie Hall; Fran Idziak; Meredith Andrews; Jedd Medefind; Andy Lehman; Hayley Catt; Tom Davis; Bill & Michelle McConomy; Dr. Brad Davidson; Dr. Jamie Dew; Dr. Milton Sevilla; Steve & Laura Gage; Sabrina Freeland; Kristi Fields, Debbie Meredith and the quilting group; Eve Nemitz & the Lalapalooza Co-op; Dr. Daniel Akin; Dr. Mark Liederbach; Dr. Dwayne Milioni; Mark Armstrong; Dr. Susan Hillis; Shawnda Kovacs; Don & Laura Bowen; Tom Klema; Saxon & Shannon Williams.

A very special thank you to Dr. James Dobson and *Focus on the Family*. The Lord has used this ministry to help reconcile and nurture our marriage; for me to be a stay at home, homeschool mom; provide wisdom and encouragement in raising our children; and in our adoption journey. Dr. Dobson, I am forever grateful to you for your love and obedience to the Lord Jesus Christ. I and my family have been blessed more than I can write here by your faithfulness in this ministry.

A special thank you to Dennis Rainey and *FamilyLife Today®,* a ministry of Campus Crusade. We are forever grateful for your faithfulness and have been blessed and encouraged in nurturing our marriage, raising our children, and in our adoption journey and ministry. We are a family that has been nurtured and blessed more than words can express here by your faithfulness in this ministry.

We are forever grateful to each and every one of you who have poured into our lives with love, prayer, and support to help make us the family we are today! May the Lord pour His blessings upon you!

And to you, the reader, thank you for taking time out of your busy life to read tHIS journey of faith. I pray it will encourage you to be filled with hope and encouragement, and that you will be drawn to seek the Lord Jesus Christ for your own life and be inspired to make a difference in the life of an orphan. May you be blessed and seek His will for your life!

In HIS TIMING & CARE,

With Love,

Eileen

About the Author

Eileen Mestas and her husband, Jerry, have been married for thirty-three years and live in Wake Forest, North Carolina. They had three biological children and were living the American dream, headed toward the empty nest, until God radically transformed their lives by awakening their hearts to the orphan crisis. They have since adopted five children, both domestic and international. They served in ministry to the Kolfe Boys Orphanage in Ethiopia, which resulted in another unofficially adopted son who came to the USA as an international student. Eileen is an inventor and patent owner[1], an author, public speaker, and a passionate Adoption and Orphan Care advocate. She spends most of her days homeschooling their children and juggling the duties of being a privileged wife, stay-at-home mom, and grandmother to her three grandchildren, as well as caring for her mom who lives with them. Most importantly, she is a born-again Christian who loves the Lord Jesus and desires to serve Him with her life.

1. Patent US5652958 - A Nursing canopy for use by a nursing mother to maintain privacy and modesty in public. (www.google.com/patents/US5652958)

Contact Information

Additional copies of this book can be ordered from your favorite retail or online bookseller.

For additional information about having Eileen speak at your event, or for autographed copies of the book, please visit:

www.MoreThanICanHandle.com

Or contact:

Mustard Seed Faith Ministries
P.O. Box 1862
Wake Forest, NC 27587
(919) 671-6482
eileenmestas@gmail.com